I0817561

GREAT MYSTERIES OF THE UNEXPLAINED

GREAT MYSTERIES OF THE UNEXPLAINED

EXTRAORDINARY TALES OF STRANGE PHENOMENA

ANDREW HOLLAND,
LUCY DONCASTER AND KAREN FARRINGTON

CONTENTS

Introduction. 6

Chapter 1

DISAPPEARANCES 8

Lord Lucan 10
Agatha Christie 12
Dr Leon Theremin 14
The Vanished Battalion 16
D. B. Cooper. 20
Amelia Earhart 24
The *Mary Celeste* 28
Flight 19 32
USS *Cyclops* 36
Glenn Miller 38

Chapter 2

LOST WORLDS AND MYSTERIOUS MONUMENTS 40

The Dogon. 42
Ciudad Blanca 46
The Anasazi. 48
The Moche 50
The Age of the Pharaohs . . . 52
Baalbeck. 56
Newgrange 58
Stonehenge. 60
Atlantis. 64
Yonaguni 68
The Nazca Lines 72
The Arthur Stone 76

SIRIUS

This edition published in 2025 by Sirius Publishing, a division of Arcturus Publishing Limited,
26/27 Bickels Yard, 151–153 Bermondsey Street,
London SE1 3HA

ISBN: 978-1-3988-5183-2
AD012483UK

Printed in Malaysia

Chapter 3

PARANORMAL POWERS 80

Eileen Garrett. 82
Helen Duncan. 86
Eusapia Palladino 88
Madame Blavatsky 90
Noreen Renier 96
Jeane Dixon. 100
Ninel Kulagina 102
Daniel Dunglas Home. 104
Jose Arigo. 108
The Girl with X-Ray Eyes. . . . 110

Chapter 4

SEERS AND ORACLES 114

The Delphic Oracle 116
Nostradamus 118
The Sangoma. 122
The Brahan Seer 124
Edgar Cayce, the
Sleeping Prophet. 128
Titanic Predictions 132
The Unknown Prophet 134
The Hitler Horoscopes 138
Gordon Scallion 140

Chapter 5

CURSES 142

The Power of Curses 144
The Little Bastard 150
Chief Cornstalk 154
The Black Hope Curse 158
The Earls of Mar 162

Chapter 6

CREATURES OF MYSTERY 166

Sounds of the Deep. 168
Kraken 170
Lake Monsters 174
Bunyip 180
Nandi Bears 182
Orang-Pendek 184
Kongamato 186
Mokele-mbembe 190
The Venezuelan Apeman . . . 192
Chupacabra 196
Jersey Devil. 198
Skinwalkers 202

Index 206
Picture Credits. 208

INTRODUCTION

The world is full of unexplained mysteries and we can only speculate as to what might have caused these remarkable events.

The world is full of things we can't explain. There are people who vanish without a trace, the remains of ancient civilizations which speak to a fantastical past, men and women who hold powers unable to be explained by science, individuals who predict the future, rumours of dark curses and mysterious creatures roaming the wilderness, to name just a few.

The famous science fiction author Arthur C. Clarke once wrote that 'any sufficiently advanced technology is indistinguishable from magic.' So while many of these mysteries seem impossible to solve to us today, it may be that the true explanation is lurking just around the corner, waiting for our knowledge to advance sufficiently for understanding to be possible.

Some mysteries turn out to be elaborate hoaxes. Others may owe their existence to the strange quirks of the human mind or rare natural phenomenon. Yet it is possible that extraterrestrial influences or paranormal forces may be at work too – and we should not be too quick to rule out such explanations.

Phenomena such as lightning, hieroglyphics, and the existence of a Northwest Passage were considered as unsolved mysteries, yet each in turn revealed their secrets when given sufficient attention and the advance of technology.

This book explores some of the most remarkable and curious mysteries of the world that we have yet to find a satisfying explanation for. Ranging from the travels of the ghost ship the *Mary Celeste* to the cryptic yet surprisingly accurate prophecies of Nostradamus, it explores in detail the unnatural occurrences themselves, the people involved, those who sought to investigate and solve the mysteries and the wider contexts in which such mysteries evolve.

The number of unexplained mysteries out there is almost countless, and each unique in its own way, but there are some common categories where strange occurrences crop up time and again. In this book, we have divided the cases into six of the most common categories:

- **Disappearances** – For millennia, there have been accounts of men and women suddenly vanishing, with no explanation of their whereabouts or how they could have gone missing. The answer may be simple human malevolence at play, or something altogether more mysterious.

- **Lost Worlds and Mysterious Monuments** – the world is full of the remains of ancient civilizations of which we only have the barest understanding. Their monuments litter the landscape, but how did they build such extraordinary structures? And what was their purpose?

- **Paranormal Powers** – throughout history, some individuals have been gifted with extraordinary powers that cannot be explained by the science of the day. What should we make of these? Are those who claim to have such powers astonishingly gifted hoaxers, or are their purported powers real – and if so, what does that tell us about the world we live in?

- **Seers and Oracles** – Are there really people out there able out there with the ability to predict the future?

- **Curses** – throughout human history, there have been accounts of some people using supernatural powers to inflict a curse on those they believe have wronged them. These magical afflictions can last for generations, leaving families to suffer ill luck, loss of wealth and sometimes even death.

- **Creatures of Mystery** – there is no shortage of reports of sightings of giant mysterious creatures – known as 'cryptids' – from amateur adventurers. Ranging from the Loch Ness monster to giant apemen like the Yeti, these beasts seem both terrifying and wondrous to those who encounter them.

Within the pages ahead, you are sure to learn about things that you had never imagined possible. Whether you would prefer to simply enjoy tales of the strange world around us or wish to play amateur sleuth and pose your own explanations for these events, the mysteries ahead are sure to hold your attention.

CHAPTER 1
DISAPPEA

RANCES

Every day, all over the world, people go missing – either of their own volition, or due to circumstances beyond their control. When a person in the public eye disappears, such as Lord Lucan or Agatha Christie, the case grips the public imagination, with sightings of the missing person being reported from all quarters. Speculation about the motivation behind these events rages, although the truth of the matter is often never discovered.

When an area has a history of repeated vanishings, such as the Bermuda Triangle, the possibility of some sort of extra-terrestrial intervention inspires fevered speculation. But disappearances of any sort leave unsolved mysteries and unanswered questions.

LORD LUCAN

The disappearance of Lord Lucan has perplexed the nation and confounded the law for decades. There are many unanswered questions concerning the crimes from which he fled and, thirty years later, the mystery is no nearer to being solved.

Until the time of his vanishing, Lord Lucan lived the life of a typical English aristocrat. After leaving boarding school, he embarked upon a short career in the armed forces. This was followed by a brief stint in merchant banking before he turned his hand to his main passion in life – gambling. In this, he displayed an obvious affinity with risk-taking. In fact, he enjoyed such success that he earned himself the nickname of 'Lucky', and, to the consternation of his wife, took up gambling as a profession.

However, as time went on, Lucan's luck appeared to change and he accrued a large tally of gambling debts

Lord Lucan works on the engine of his powerboat in 1963. Before his disappearance, he lived the life of an ordinary English aristocrat.

Police officers searched the area around Newhaven after they found his car abandoned nearby. Lord Lucan was the prime suspect in the cases of the murder of Sandra Rivett and the attempted murder of Lady Lucan, but he was never found.

that threatened the financial security of his children. It was this, together with other factors, which led to the breakdown of his marriage and the ensuing bitter custody battle between the estranged couple.

On 7 November 1974, matters went from bad to worse. In Lucan's family home in London, two crimes took place – the murder of the children's nanny, Sandra Rivett, and the attempted murder of his wife. Accounts of the events which took place on this night vary as much as the many theories that attempt to explain what happened. However, the identity of the prime suspect for both of these crimes is something upon which all seemed to agree – Lord Lucan himself.

After the crimes took place, Lucan gave his own personal account to friends. He stated that an assailant had entered the house and brutally attacked his wife, leaving her hysterical and bleeding profusely. Lucan had interrupted the assault and wrestled with the attacker, slipping during the struggle in the blood that covered the floor. Realizing that he had thus unwittingly implicated himself in the attack, he reasoned that he would have difficulty in proving his innocence, and decided to flee.

In opposition to this is the report given by Lady Lucan, which was supported by an inquiry. In this, she claimed that Lucan had intended to murder her that night, but that the attempt had gone wrong and he had killed the nanny by mistake. Lady Lucan stated that she herself had fought with her ex-husband, and had been lucky to escape with her life. Her injuries appeared to support this story, but was her assailant actually her husband?

A third theory that has been put forward is that Lucan had hired a hit man to kill his wife, but that the supposed assassin had mistakenly murdered Sandra Rivett instead, as the two women were of a similar build. Lucan then attempted to dispose of Rivett's body, but on being disturbed by his wife had tried to murder her, in line with the original plan.

Many believe that the fact that Lucan fled the scene of the crime and abandoned his distressed wife is proof of his culpability. Since Lucan's disappearance, there have been many unofficial reported sightings of this elusive fugitive all over the world. This has served only to deepen the sense of mystery surrounding this particular case, and it seems likely that unless he surfaces, the truth of the crime and how he managed to vanish without trace may never be known.

It is somehow fitting that Agatha Christie, the undisputed queen of mystery writing, should have been involved in her own mysterious event – her sudden, unexplained disappearance. Although only temporary, this occurrence has never been properly explained. What were the reasons behind the event, which could easily have come straight out of one of her own elaborate murder stories?

Christie disappeared on the evening of Friday 3 December 1926. When asked by the police to provide an alibi, her husband Archie was forced to admit that he had spent the weekend with his mistress. This information led police to suspect that Archie may have had a motive for murder, or that she may have taken her own life.

A wide-ranging search began immediately and, the next day, her abandoned car was discovered, strewn with her clothes and belongings. The vehicle was located near both a quarry and a lake, fuelling suspicion that Christie may have committed suicide. Coincidentally, the lake had actually featured in one of her crime novels as the site of a drowning. In light of these factors, the police had the lake dredged, but they found nothing.

The search was then widened to the surrounding countryside, with thousands of volunteers drafted in. This also proved fruitless. Then, after a few days of press publicity, Christie was identified as being alive and well in a health spa in Yorkshire, where she was staying under an assumed name.

£27,500,000 PLAN FOR EASING LONDON'S TRAFFIC

Daily Mirror

THE DAILY PICTURE NEWSPAPER WITH THE LARGEST NET SALE

No. 7,201 THURSDAY, DECEMBER 9, 1926 One Penny

PREMIER AND "HYSTERICAL" MR. COOK

NOVELIST MYSTERY

VAIN FIGHT FOR ACTRESS'S LIFE

NEWS PORTRAITS

The Daily Mirror *reports on Agatha Christie's mysterious disappearance.*

AGATHA CHRISTIE

The official explanation was that Christie had been suffering from amnesia, brought on by the death of her mother. This, however, sounded more like a fabrication than anything grounded in reality, and the public remained mystified.

Christie never revealed her actions or motives to anyone, and as she died in 1976, it is unlikely that we shall ever know the truth. She made no mention of the episode in her memoirs and, whenever asked about her disappearance, she never wavered from the amnesia story.

Over the years, there has been much speculation about the possible reasons for what happened. Could it have been an act of revenge on Christie's adulterous husband, or the symptoms of a nervous breakdown, or even a cleverly constructed publicity stunt? Whatever the reasons, the event can only enhance her reputation as a true mistress of the unexplained.

Agatha Christie in 1926.

Leon Theremin playing his revolutionary musical instrument.

DR LEON THEREMIN

The peculiar disappearance of the scientist and inventor Dr Leon Theremin is thought to have more to do with the shady world of international espionage than with any other possible cause. It seems likely that Theremin vanished in order to work for the Kremlin and thus further the Soviet cause, but whether this was of his own choosing, or whether he was coerced into doing so, is a matter for speculation.

Dr Theremin arrived in the USA in 1927, bearing his original Russian name, Lev Sergeyevich Termen. His particular area of expertise was radio electronics, and it did not take him long to put these skills to commercial use. After spending some time working on a revolutionary musical instrument, he successfully obtained a patent for it, and it became known as the 'Theremin'. The way in which this strange instrument is played is totally unprecedented, since sounds are created by moving the hands around two radio antennae rather than by any physical contact with the machine.

The eerie notes emitted by this instrument resulted in its use in a number of films of the time, including those of Alfred Hitchcock, in which the sounds were used to create suspense. The effect of this was to raise Dr Theremin's public profile and he began to enjoy a kind of celebrity status in the USA. This fame, however, may have proved to be a double-edged sword, as whilst Theremin enjoyed the fruits of his success, those with sinister intentions became aware of how this talented scientist could assist them in their schemes and plans.

It was Theremin's experiments in the field of radio waves and frequencies, and subsequent creation of the first radio surveillance 'bug', which are thought to have sealed his fate. In 1938 the inventor went missing, and after a while he was presumed to be dead.

It eventually transpired that Theremin had left his house in 1938 in the company of several Soviet agents, who accompanied him back to his homeland. Here, he was thought to have worked for the Soviets on espionage devices and security systems. It is unclear whether or not he was in fact kidnapped, but it seems unlikely that he would have voluntarily exchanged his successful life in New York for the Siberian labour camp in which he ended up.

Many questions about this intelligent man remain unanswered. Was Theremin really interested in using his skills to further the demands of the Cold War powers? This seems unlikely and, although trained in the field of science, when given the choice, Theremin applied himself instead to the peaceful development of music.

Theremin's unexplained disappearance was one of the many curious incidents that have since been attributed to the Soviet authorities during the Cold War. The incredible paranoia and secrecy of that period has left many lasting mysteries. Only now, years after the era ended, are we finding even small clues as to the truth of what actually went on at that time.

THE VANISHED

When a person disappears, a range of possible reasons for what has happened spring to mind. Did the missing person suffer some kind of mental breakdown? Did they take their own life? Or could they even have been kidnapped? These are the most obvious explanations. When, however, a large number of people vanish together, without trace, the usual assumptions become less valid.

When a group of people disappears on land, rather than in the air or at sea, the occurrence becomes even more perplexing. The sea will always hold a certain mystique and is easily capable of hiding the evidence if lives have been lost there. This is much harder to do on land, however, and it is thus truly remarkable that, in 1915, no fewer than 250 British soldiers and 16 officers simply disappeared from a battlefield in the Dardanelles region of Turkey.

Although well known for its scrupulous record keeping, the military was, and is, unable to shed any light on what might have happened. Furthermore, the strong adherence to the laws that prevent desertion would seem to preclude the idea of these men trying

The beach at Gallipoli containing the British encampment. The Fifth Territorial Battalion of the Royal Norfolk Regiment vanished just two days after arriving at the battle.

BATTALION

to escape their duties. It is very unlikely that more than a few of the officers spoke the local language, and anyone captured deserting would have been shot as an example to others. In addition to this, the men who disappeared were formed from the staff of the King's Sandringham estate. Undoubtedly, this would have been a source of great honour to them and not something that they would have discarded lightly.

The men in question had formed E company of the Fifth Territorial Battalion of the Royal Norfolk Regiment, which had been formed in 1908 at the personal behest of King Edward VII. More informally, however, the soldiers were known as 'The Sandringhams'. These men would all have known each other well, both through their work on the estate and due to the fact that they had all grown up together in the same area.

Prior to the outbreak of war, the company consisted of just over 100 part-time territorial soldiers, but after hostilities began more men from the area joined up voluntarily. In those days, military rank would have been decided by social class rather than on any martial merit, with the members of the local gentry forming the ranks of officers. The middle-ranking soldiers, the non-commissioned officers (NCOs), would have been chosen from workers such as the butlers, foremen and gamekeepers, while the rank and file of the troops would have consisted of the labourers and servants from the royal estate.

Despite their lack of experience, the men were keen to engage with the enemy and, after their initial training, they were taken to Turkey to participate in the battle at Gallipoli. They were led into this first engagement by their commanding officer, Colonel Horace Proctor Beauchamp, who would have been eager for his company to make its name on the battlefield.

The last sighting of the missing men occurred on 12 August 1915, just two days after they had arrived at the conflict. They had been given the order to advance on a position that was held by the Turks about 2km (1.2 miles) away. The position was well defended and they had to attack in broad daylight with little in the way of cover. As the troops advanced, Colonel Beauchamp led from the front and harried his men to press the assault. The soldiers are believed to have driven ahead further than the rest of the main assault and may have become cut off from them. They were last sighted entering some woods near the Turkish position, in disarray, and obscured by smoke and clouds.

When the battle was over it was realized that the entire group of men was missing. Despite the horrendous rate of casualties in World War I, it was unusual for there to be no survivors at all. Enquiries were made to ascertain whether any of them were being held in Turkish prisoner-of-war camps, but this was proven not to be the case. How, then, could this many men have simply disappeared, literally, in a cloud of smoke?

Is it possible that the reason behind the battalion's disappearance lies within the realms of the paranormal? In 1965, at the 50th anniversary of the fateful Gallipoli landings, a former New Zealand sapper, Frederick Reichardt, claimed that he had witnessed a strange event that could explain what had happened. This account was supported by three other veterans, who all asserted that something out of the ordinary had taken place on the battlefield.

Reichardt stated that he and his fellow soldiers had witnessed the Sandringhams' heroic charge into the woods, whereupon they seemed to rush headlong into a peculiar formation of about eight loaf-shaped clouds which were lying at ground level over the area.

The soldiers were seen to enter the clouds, but never appeared again. Reichardt states that, after about an hour, the clouds rose up into the sky, leaving no trace of the soldiers of the Norfolk battalion.

Whether this explanation has any basis in reality is open to speculation. There are some who would argue that perhaps some kind of religious intervention had taken place. This was the battalion's first engagement, and so none of them had yet been bloodied by the carnage. Perhaps they had been spirited away to heaven before they had had a chance to become sullied by the horrors of war.

Others view the story of the clouds as evidence of an extra-terrestrial abduction. This seems to tie in with some of the descriptions given when ships and aircraft disappear, as they often vanish into cloudy skies. It should be remembered, however, that heavy clouds are an indication of poor weather conditions, which could explain the disappearances.

A third suggestion is that the clouds seen on the battlefield were not due to atmospheric conditions at all, but were in fact palls of smoke emanating from the intense fire and bombardment of the battlefield. As such, then, the soldiers had not disappeared at all, but had simply been killed. This seems unlikely, however, as there are very few military engagements in which there are no survivors whatsoever.

A fourth and final possibility is believed by many historians to be the most likely explanation, although perhaps this is because they are unwilling

Reichardt claimed that the Sandringhams had charged headlong into a formation of loaf-shaped clouds. It is possible that these clouds were nothing more than the smoke from artillery fire.

to countenance some of the other, more unusual, theories. The suggestion put forward is linked to the brutal reputation of the battalion's Turkish opponents, who were renowned for taking no prisoners. If they did happen to hold any soldiers captive, it was usually only for a very brief period, before they then executed them en masse. In support of this theory, a large number of corpses was found buried on the battlefield in the following years, with execution-style gunshot wounds to the head. Could the peculiar disappearance of all these men be attributed simply to a mass murder?

Similar crimes had been committed before on the battlefield, as history will attest. It is entirely possible that the Turks may have found themselves threatened by the sheer numbers of their own captives, and thus may have executed the men for their own safety.

Although the disappearance of these men is shrouded in mystery, it is certainly not the only occasion on which soldiers of the Great War have gone missing in action. The incredible levels of carnage on the battlefields of Europe meant that many thousands of men remained unaccounted for after battle, with bodies rendered unrecognizable due to the scale of the bloodshed. What sets this mystery apart from others, however, is the fact that all the men vanished together, never to be heard of again. It is a mystery that has perplexed historians for generations, and will no doubt continue to do so until some breakthrough evidence is found.

A Boeing 727 of the type hijacked by D. B. Cooper.

An FBI sketch of D. B. Cooper from 1973.

D. B. COOPER

The disappearance of D. B. Cooper on 24 November 1971 is an interesting tale. This criminal managed to evade the law after hijacking a commercial airliner and then parachuting from it into oblivion, taking with him a large sum of money that he had received as a ransom payment.

What remains a mystery is how Cooper ever managed to escape from the vast operation mounted to secure his capture. The area in which his parachute would have come down is a huge, remote forest that was covered with a thick blanket of snow at the time. More than 300 Federal Bureau of Investigation (FBI) agents spent over a month combing the area for any evidence of Cooper, but none was ever found.

The hijacking of aircraft was a remarkably common occurrence between 1967 and 1972, with more than 150 taking place during this period. Generally, however, hijacks were carried out for political motives. Cooper was the first person to exploit the weakness of air security for his own financial gain.

In planning the operation, Cooper had been particular about his choice of aircraft, ensuring that the one he boarded was a Boeing 727. The reason for this was that the 727 was the only passenger airliner with steps that lowered from a hatch at the very rear of the aircraft, beneath the tail. This hatch would allow Cooper to make his daring escape by parachute. Later, all 727s were modified to prevent such an attempt being made again.

Cooper began his elaborate stunt by purchasing a one-way ticket from Seattle to Tacoma on Northwest Airlines flight 305. Although barely half-full, the flight contained more than enough hostages for Cooper's needs. While the aircraft was still on the tarmac at Seattle, he handed a stewardess a note setting out his demands for US$200,000 in unmarked bills, four parachutes and, reportedly, 'no funny stuff'.

Unfortunately, the stewardess mistook the note for a proposition of some kind, and failed to read it until the aircraft was airborne. When she then confronted Cooper, he responded by showing her the contents of his bag, which appeared to resemble a bomb.

At this point, the 727 changed its course and returned to Seattle where the FBI was waiting. Rather than storm the aircraft, it complied with Cooper's demands for the ransom and parachutes, having first taken note of the serial numbers of all 10,000 of the $20 bills. It could not run the risk of tampering with the parachutes as it could not be certain that Cooper would not take hostages with him.

Having received what he had asked for, Cooper then demanded that the aircraft be flown to Mexico. To enable him to make his jump, he insisted on certain conditions being met: the aircraft was to fly with its

Some of the $20 bills stolen by Cooper.

NORTHWEST ORIENT
PASSENGER TICKET AND BAGGAGE CHECK
FLIGHT COUPON NO. 1
NOT TRANSFERABLE
NAME OF PASSENGER: DAN COOPER
DATE OF ISSUE: 11 24 71
AIRLINE FORM SERIAL NUMBER: 012 14 4406773
PORTLAND
FROM: PTLND ORE 91852
TO: SEATTLE
Y NW 305 Y 11/24 245P OK
FARE 18 52
TAX 1 48
TOTAL 20.00
1 012 144406773 0
USED NOV 24 '71 305
IT IS UNLAWFUL TO PURCHASE OR RESELL THIS TICKET FROM/TO ANY SOURCE OTHER THAN NORTHWEST AIRLINES OR ITS AUTHORIZED TRAVEL AGENT.

The ticket bought under the name 'Dan Cooper' for the flight to Seattle.

landing gear and flaps down, in order to slow its progress; its speed was not to exceed 273 km/h (170 mph); and its altitude was to be restricted to 3,048m (10,000ft).

Complying with these conditions, the pilots realized that they would not be able to reach Mexico without refuelling, and so informed Cooper that they would have to land at Reno. Cooper agreed to this without complaint. In hindsight, it appears that he had never intended to go to Mexico after all.

The aircraft then departed for Reno, but shortly after take-off the crew, who had been confined to the front cabin away from Cooper, noticed the flashing of a warning indicator light, showing that Cooper had opened the rear hatch. About ten minutes later, at 8.11 pm, the crew felt pressure bumps, suggesting that Cooper had made his jump. He was never seen again.

It seemed that Cooper was not only an extraordinary escape artist, but that he was also blessed with exceptional powers of endurance, since the conditions into which he had jumped were abominable. Wearing only a suit, shoes and a parachute, he had leapt from a considerable height directly into a snowstorm. The temperature at 3,048m (10,000ft) was estimated to be -22°C outside the aircraft, with a wind chill factor of -57°C.

Even if he had survived such a descent (which is possible as it would have taken less than a minute), Cooper still had to land safely in a forest in complete darkness and then find his way out without dying of exposure or being caught by the authorities.

The FBI launched a huge operation, using every available resource, to try to find Cooper. They calculated the search area by assessing information from the flight crew, which gave them a rough idea of where he might have landed. Attempts were also made to pursue the aircraft in both fixed-wing aircraft and helicopters and a massive search on the ground was mounted. No evidence of Cooper was ever found, and the FBI remained baffled by his escape.

The mystery was to deepen almost a decade later, on the other side of the country. In February 1980 in Vancouver, Washington, a boy named Brian Ingram uncovered a portion of the money while digging a hole in a riverbank. The notes were not in good condition, but it was possible to discern the serial numbers, which matched some of those used in the ransom payment. However, the location and quantity of notes found simply created further confusion among the authorities. As well as being a great distance away from the area where Cooper had jumped, Ingram had discovered only US$5,800 of the original US$200,000.

Even though this find suggests that Cooper, or at least part of the ransom, survived, really all that the world is left with is a series of questions. Where is Cooper now? Where is the remaining US$194,200? Was the money buried in Washington to act as a decoy? Did Cooper fool everyone by jumping at a different moment to what was thought, and in so doing ruin the FBI's calculations? Did he have an accomplice waiting for him? Whatever the answers, Cooper's daring feat remains one of the most perplexing and infamous unsolved crimes to this day.

This bag contained one of the parachutes Cooper used to jump from the plane.

The spirited aviatrix had achieved everything she wanted in life, but she yearned to take on one more big challenge.

AMELIA EARHART

Amelia Earhart was a pioneer, both in terms of aviation and in the advancement of women's rights. Not only was she one of the first women to be issued with a pilot's licence by the FAI (Federation Aeronautique Internationale) in America in 1923, but she also went on to break several aviation records in the years that followed, earning herself a prodigious reputation. No wonder, then, that her failure to return from a record-breaking attempt in 1937 was the most high-profile disappearance of the time, and remains as much a mystery today as it was then.

One of Earhart's greatest accomplishments took place in 1932, when she became the first woman to fly across the Atlantic. In doing so, she also set a new record of 13 hours and 30 minutes of continuous flying, despite the fact that the journey had almost ended in tragedy on more than one occasion, with Earhart being beset by several major setbacks. The first of these was a serious lightning storm that almost caused her to crash into the Atlantic. Then, as she approached the coast of Europe, she realized that her aircraft was leaking fuel and she was forced to make an emergency landing in a field in Ireland. In spite of these challenges, Earhart successfully completed the flight and her name entered the history books.

Having crossed the Atlantic, Earhart decided to

Earhart standing in front of the Lockheed Electra plane which she used for her final flight in 1937.

go one step further. In 1935 she flew across the Pacific from Hawaii to California. This feat also ended in triumph and, her confidence boosted, Earhart began to plan an airborne circumnavigation of the globe at its widest point – the Equator. The trip was too difficult and perilous for anyone, even Earhart, to attempt alone, so she asked Fred Noonan to accompany her as a navigator.

Earhart and Noonan were last seen when they took off from Lae, New Guinea, on the most treacherous leg of the flight. At this point they were just two days and around 11,000km (5,940 nautical miles) away from completing the courageous journey. Their destination was a tiny piece of land in the Pacific known as Howland Island.

Although the weather conditions had been good when the pair left Lae, the sky rapidly became overcast, disrupting navigation. However, Earhart and Noonan still had support, in the form of radio contact with the Coast Guard cutter *Itasca*. Then, at 7.42am on 2 July 1937, the *Itasca* received a message from Earhart stating: 'cannot see you, gas is running low, been unable to reach you by radio, we are flying at 1,000 feet [sic]... one half-hour fuel and no landfall'.

The *Itasca* responded by creating a beacon of thick black smoke and ordering all ships in the area to switch on every light available to assist the stricken aircraft. Earhart managed to make one final contact with the ship, in which she gave her assumed position. This was effectively the last that was ever heard of her.

In an effort to try to locate Earhart and Noonan, the USA launched the largest search and rescue operation that had ever been attempted. Unfortunately, in spite of combing vast areas of ocean, the search teams failed to locate the pair, and abandoned their quest.

The flyers were reported as missing, presumed dead, and the world could only guess at what had happened to them. To add to the mystery, sightings of the famous pair were made long after the search

Lae, New Guinea. It was from here that Earhart began the final, and most treacherous portion, of her voyage.

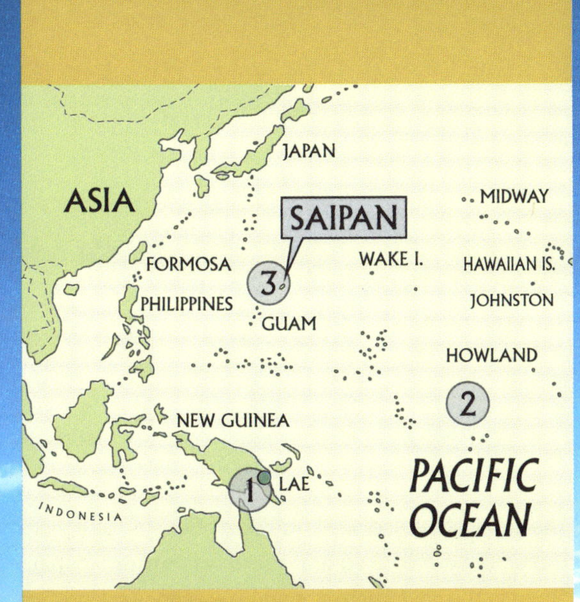

A map of Earhart's route shows how she may have ended up on the island of Saipan. Could she have been a US agent, spying on the Japanese?

had been concluded. In his 1987 book, *Eyewitness: the Amelia Earhart Incident*, Thomas E. Devine (a former American GI) claimed that the pair had been spotted alive and well on the Japanese-held island of Saipan during World War II. Following the publication of this book, several other GIs came forward to corroborate the story, lending it some credence.

However, when Saipan was invaded by the US in 1944, no trace of the pilot and her navigator was ever found. All that is known for sure is that Amelia Earhart and Fred vanished somewhere over the Pacific Ocean on 2 July 1937. No one can be certain how two such experienced flyers could disappear under such circumstances, or why their radio seemed to fail at such a crucial moment. Unless further evidence comes to light, these questions will remain unanswered and people will continue to speculate over what really happened to these two courageous aviators.

THE *MARY CELESTE*

A ship bobbing on the open seas, its crew inexplicably missing, sails flapping aimlessly in the wind. A search aboard reveals no trace of life, and few clues as to what might have occurred. The story of the *Mary Celeste* is one of history's most intriguing mysteries.

On 7 November 1872, Captain Benjamin Spooner Briggs sailed out of New York. He was bound for Genoa, Italy on what should have been a workaday voyage. With him was his wife Sarah, 30, their two-year-old daughter Sophia Matilda, and a capable crew of two Americans, one Dane, one German and three Dutchmen. In the hold of the half-brig *Mary Celeste* was a cargo of 1,700 barrels of alcohol intended for wine fortification.

After she left New York there were no further reports of her progress until 5 December, when the ship *Dei Gratia*, loaded with petroleum, spotted her between the Azores and the Portuguese coast. As it happened, the captain of the *Dei Gratia*, David Morehouse, was one of Briggs' personal friends, and the pair had dined together shortly before Briggs left New York. Morehouse noted the erratic progress of the *Mary Celeste* and tried to make contact for some time before dispatching a boarding party.

Led by Chief Mate Oliver Deveau, the merchant seamen climbed aboard the erring ship. But it quickly became clear that the *Mary Celeste* was completely deserted, and there were few clues as to why. The chronometer and sextant were missing but the log book was in its place. Hatches were open but the crews' oilskins were still there. The lifeboat was gone, although food and water supplies were intact, as were the barrels. The galley stove had been dislodged. Belongings aboard the ship were soaked and there was water sloshing about in the hold where one pump was not working. But the ship was, to all intents and purposes, still seaworthy. Ignoring the sinister atmosphere aboard the mystery ship, some hardy members of the crew from the *Dei Gratia* sailed her into Gibraltar. Reading the last entry in the ship's log, Morehouse learnt that the *Mary Celeste* had passed 10km (5.4 nautical miles) from St Mary's in the Azores at 8am on 25 November, some ten days earlier. Just what happened between that day and the discovery of the empty ship may never be discovered. Theories about the possible fate of those aboard have abounded.

Suspicions that it was some manner of insurance scam have been dispelled. Briggs was a devout man with a solid reputation. Likewise, there is nothing to indicate a mutiny among the crew, who were all experienced men well used to short commercial voyages such as these.

One man, having examined the calamity in depth, felt he had touched on the correct explanation. Charles Edey Fay made a detailed study of the oddities surrounding the discovery of the *Mary Celeste*. He concluded that Briggs had probably taken advantage of unexpectedly calm conditions to ventilate the cargo. In fact, nine barrels of the alcohol had leaked, causing noxious fumes to pour out of the hold. In the chaos that ensued, perhaps it seemed as if an explosion was imminent or that the ship was sinking.

Briggs, who had never carried alcohol before and was religiously opposed to its very existence, may well have given the order to abandon ship and take to the

The Mary Celeste *was found floating, empty but undamaged, in the sea between the Azores and the Portuguese coast.*

Abel Fosdyk claimed that during a swimming race, some members of the crew were attacked by sharks. When the others rushed to see what was happening, they fell overboard and met the same fate...

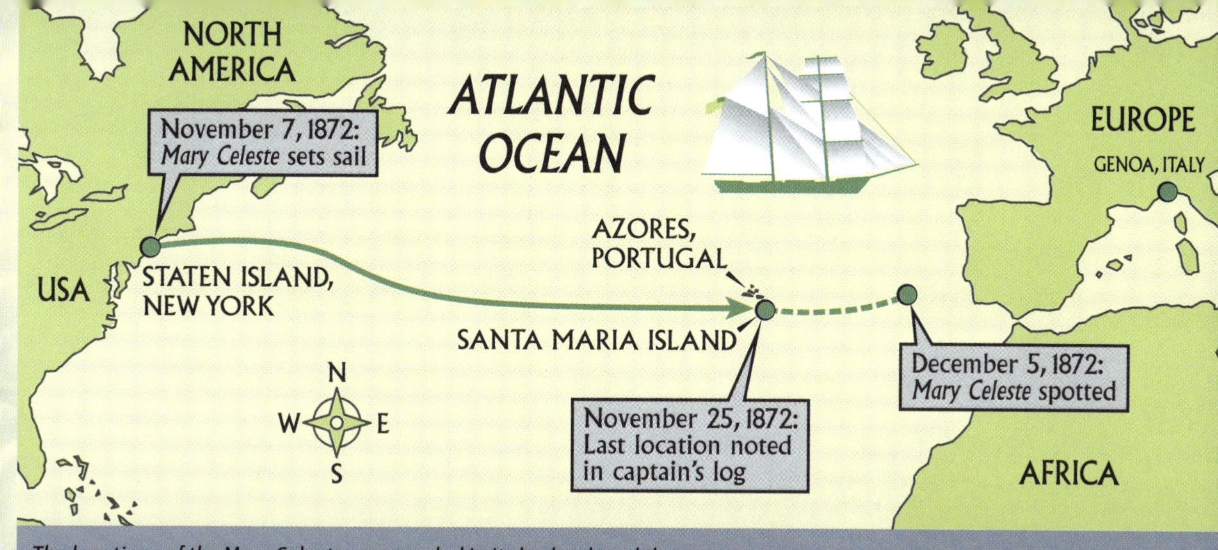

The locations of the Mary Celeste*, as recorded in its logbook and the location it was discovered in.*

lifeboat. His best option was to maintain contact with the ship through the halyard, a weighty rope. Once they felt the danger had passed, those in the lifeboat would have clambered back aboard the ship and resumed their voyage. What they had not anticipated was a change in the weather. Fay's theory is that they were surprised by a squall, and the halyard was severed, leaving the lifeboat adrift in the open.

The lifeboat would then either have sunk, or drifted in a south-easterly direction away from the land and the shipping route. Either way, its hapless occupants were doomed either to drown or to die of thirst, starvation or exposure.

A letter from the Serviço Meteorológico dos Açores confirmed that a period of calm gave way to gale force winds during that fateful night of 25 November 1872. The halyard upon which the lives of those in the lifeboat depended was found frayed over the side of the ship.

Fay's findings are outlined in *The Story of the Mary Celeste*, which he had published in 1942. His account, rooted in fact, was very different from many of the more fanciful stories inspired by the empty ship. One fictional account, published in 1883, was written by a certain Arthur Conan Doyle. He changed the name of the ship to *Marie Celeste* and asserted that everyone aboard the fated vessel came to a violent end.

The waters were further muddied by the claims of Abel Fosdyk. He claimed to have been a stowaway aboard the *Mary Celeste*, and recounted how he had watched the captain and some crew members being eaten by sharks during a swimming race. As the others rushed to witness the tragedy they all fell overboard and met the same end. Fosdyk said he clung to driftwood until being washed up on African shores. But Fosdyk wrongly identified the nationalities of all the crew, so it seems his account was also made up.

Fictional though their accounts may be, Conan Doyle and Fosdyk both helped to keep the memory of *Mary Celeste* alive. Intriguingly, she was not the only ship found abandoned at sea. In 1849, the Dutch Schooner *Hermania* was discovered dismasted and deserted. Six years later, the *Marathon* was found in a similar state, yet neither of these ships became household names.

The infamous ship was built in Nova Scotia in 1860, and was to have a brief but dramatic existence. Some accounts allude to her being an unlucky ship prior to 1872, although there are no details to support this notion. But, as the sole survivor of the 1872 disaster, she was not destined for a long life. Just a dozen years after limping into Gibraltar, she was wrecked on the rocks at Haiti. Her captain on that occasion was later punished for attempting insurance fraud.

In 2001, the coral-covered wreck of the *Mary Celeste* was located. The discovery caused ripples of excitement worldwide, but the ship's skeleton gave up no secrets, and eventually the hype subsided. The mystery of the *Mary Celeste* proved as impenetrable as it was 130 years ago.

FLIGHT 19

One of the most intriguing disappearances of all time was the loss of an entire squadron of aircraft, which vanished without trace, leaving no clue as to what had happened. The occurrence engendered much controversy, not only because there were conflicting views on the exact circumstances behind the event, but also because it kick-started the mythical reputation surrounding the area of the disappearance, the now infamous Bermuda Triangle in the Atlantic Ocean.

All kinds of explanations have been put forward in an attempt to understand the puzzle. Some blame freak weather conditions, whilst others, more bizarrely, believe that the squadron may even have been kidnapped by aliens. This theory was popularized by Stephen Spielberg in his film *Close Encounters of the Third Kind*, in which the pilots of Flight 19 were shown being returned to Earth in an alien spacecraft.

This intriguing case poses many questions. How was it possible that not one, but all five planes in a squadron, with several experts on board, could vanish so inexplicably? Even more bewildering was the fact that the search and rescue plane that was sent after them was also lost, for reasons that are still unknown.

Flight 19 – consisting of five Naval Avenger torpedo-bombers – departed Fort Lauderdale on a training flight on 5 December 1945. Each of the five planes was supposed to have had three men on board, but on the day in question, one had failed to appear, so that this flight consisted of 14 airmen in total. Of these, 13 were in the final stages of their training, although all of them were more than capable of handling their aircraft. The exercise was being led by Lt Charles Taylor, a highly experienced pilot, who had acquired much expertise in flying over the Florida Keys.

Their flight plan was to conduct a practice bombing run over an area known as the 'Hen and Chickens Shoals' that lay to the east of the Florida Keys. The squadron was then to continue to fly east over the ocean until it was around 190km (102 nautical miles) from the shore, before turning north for another 113km (61 nautical miles). It would then turn south-west and return to base. This triangular course would take the aircraft over the Bahamas, and would steer them almost continuously through the Bermuda Triangle.

A group of five Grunman TBM Avenger bombers in flight, similar to those that made up Flight 19.

The flight took off at 2.10pm in good weather, although conditions looked as if they might take a marked turn for the worse towards the evening. After less than two hours, just before 4.00pm, Fort Lauderdale received a radio transmission in which Lt Taylor stated that the squadron's compasses were not working and the pilots believed themselves to be lost. It is now known that the Bermuda Triangle is one of two areas of the world – the other being the Devil's Triangle in Asia – in which there is an unusual level of magnetic interference which can adversely affect compass readings. Could this be the reason behind the loss of so many ships and aircraft in the region?

Lt Taylor reported over the radio that he believed that the squadron was flying over the Florida Keys. He was advised that, if he was certain of this, he should direct the aircraft north towards Miami and the mainland.

If, as is thought today, Lt Taylor was mistaken and he was in fact over the Bahamas, then by flying north, Flight 19 would have taken itself further out into the Atlantic Ocean and away from safety.

No one had any reason to suspect that this was the case, however, and the squadron continued northwards. To complicate matters further, atmospheric interference from the approaching storm, coupled with the radio waves from commercial radio broadcasts in nearby Cuba, were hampering efforts to communicate with the flight. Taylor was urged to switch to the emergency frequency, which would have facilitated radio communication, but he refused. One of the aircraft was encountering problems with its radio, and Taylor feared that by changing frequencies he might lose contact with it altogether.

As time passed, the sense of urgency at the Fort Lauderdale base increased. As it was winter, the sun was due to set at around 5.30pm, and bad weather conditions were moving down from the north.

At 5.15pm, radio contact was briefly re-established, and Taylor informed the base that the flight was now heading west. He was heard advising the squadron to remain close together. The plan was that when the first aircraft ran out of fuel the remaining bombers would all ditch in the sea, thus increasing the likelihood of everyone surviving.

A Dumb seaplane, the first of several rescue aircraft, was launched shortly after 6.00pm, but rapidly lost

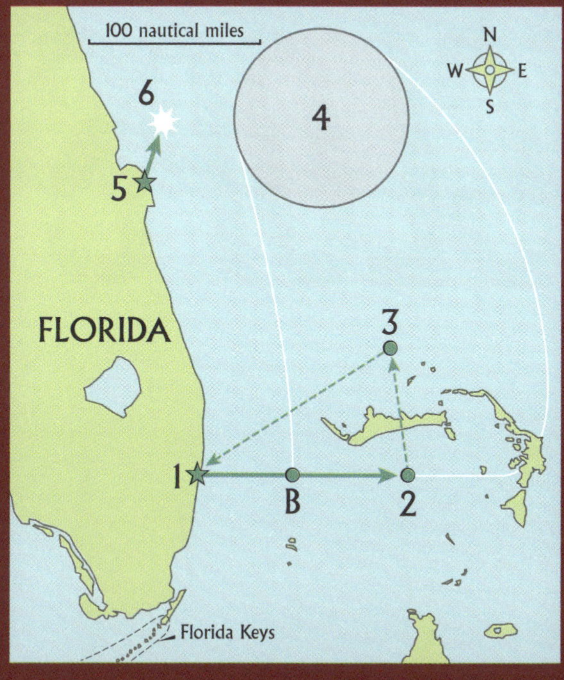

1. Leaves Fort Lauderdale at 2.10pm for 104km (56 nautical miles), drops bombs at Hens and Chickens Shoals (B) until about 3pm then continues 124km (67 nautical miles).
2. Turns left and flies 135km (73 nautical miles).
3. Turns left for 222km (120 nautical miles) to end exercise north of Fort Lauderdale.
4. 5.50pm radio triangulation establishes the flight's position to within 93km (50 nautical miles) of 29°N 79°W.
5. PBM Mariner leaves the naval station at Banana River 7.27pm.
6. 19:50 Mariner explodes near 28°N 80°W.

contact with the shore. This was attributed to the bad weather, which had caused an antenna to become iced-over. Nevertheless, it seemed that the base had lost another of its machines. A further aircraft, a Martin Mariner, was then sent after the seaplane, but, once more, radio contact was lost. Whether this was again due to the weather is unknown, but shortly after the Mariner had failed to appear at the scheduled rendezvous, the crew of a nearby ship reported sighting an aircraft that exploded. They were unable to attempt any kind of rescue as by now the conditions at sea were atrocious.

What is so baffling about this disappearance is that no survivors, bodies or debris from the lost squadron were ever found. Although the poor weather may have had a large role to play, no one could be sure of exactly what had happened, and a US Navy inquest attributed the disaster to 'causes or reasons unknown'. To this day, it is a complete mystery how an entire squadron of aircraft could simply disappear when it was so close to its home coastline.

A PBM Mariner flying boat was sent after the missing aircraft but lost radio contact too.

USS *CYCLOPS*

In its day, the USS *Cyclops* was the largest ship to serve as a collier in the US Navy's fleet, and it was capable of carrying more than 10,000 tons of cargo and in excess of 300 seamen. It seems incredible, therefore, that in March 1918 it sailed into the Bermuda Triangle and disappeared without a trace, with the loss of all hands. No distress signal was issued and the US Navy was unable to understand what had happened.

The *Cyclops* was commissioned for military service on 1 May 1917, upon America's entry into World War I. In 1918 the vessel was assigned to the Naval Overseas Transportation Service, where its main role was to refuel the British ships that were patrolling the South Atlantic, specifically the waters around Brazil. On 4 March, the *Cyclops* set sail from Barbados, bound for Norfolk, Virginia. What was to be its last complete voyage would take the ship directly through the infamous waters of the Bermuda Triangle.

When the vessel disappeared, it was originally thought that it had been torpedoed, but a search of German records after the war discounted this theory, as did the fact that no wreckage was ever found. The latter factor also made it unlikely that the ship had struck a mine. In either event, surely at least some of the crew would have been able to escape by lifeboat?

More recent attempts at explaining the tragedy have turned to the mysterious nature of the Bermuda Triangle itself. There are a number of conditions found in this area that make it a particularly treacherous place for both ships and aircraft.

Firstly, it is one of two places on Earth where compasses do not point towards true North. This can result in massive navigational errors that could spell disaster for a heavily-laden vessel such as the *Cyclops*.

To accompany this ever-present hazard are the erratic and turbulent weather patterns of the Caribbean Atlantic, which is frequently ravaged by anything from water spouts to storms and hurricanes. As if this were not enough, the currents are rapid and strong, and can not only alter the location of sandbanks, but can also drag ships on to reefs.

Another lesser-known – yet equally deadly – factor could also have caused the disappearance of the *Cyclops*. There are recorded cases of the spontaneous venting of large quantities of natural gas located under the sea, as a result of a huge build-up of pressure. This natural phenomenon can change the density of the seawater, causing any nearby vessel to sink in an instant. Without further proof, however, it is difficult to be sure whether this was the reason behind the disappearance of the *Cyclops*.

In a further strange twist, the *Cyclops*' three sister ships – the *Nereus*, the *Proteus* and the *Jupiter* – all met with unhappy endings. The *Nereus* and *Proteus* both served as colliers in World War II and were sunk by U-boats in the Atlantic, with the loss of all hands. The *Jupiter*, re-named the *Langley* and converted into the US Navy's first aircraft-carrier, was sunk by the Japanese off the coast of Java in 1942. Chillingly, all four members of this nautical family now lie somewhere at the bottom of the ocean, having claimed more than 1,000 lives among them.

What really happened in the case of the *Cyclops* is almost impossible to determine due to the lack of evidence of any sort. As it is not known exactly where the ship went down, it is almost impossible to hunt for a wreck, and until such time as any telltale scraps of wreckage are found, there will only ever be theories. Thus the tragic fate of the *Cyclops*, the largest US Navy vessel ever to have disappeared inexplicably, remains a mystery.

A picture of USS Cyclops, taken shortly before she mysteriously disappeared in 1918.

Glenn Miller was an accomplished musician and leader of one of the most successful bands of the era. On his way to Paris in 1944 he suddenly disappeared.

GLENN MILLER

Glenn Miller not only enjoyed great acclaim as a musician and entertainer, but also served as an officer in the US Air Force during World War II. His successful combination of the two roles earned him great respect and he played a large part in boosting the morale of the Allied troops during the conflict.

So it was a huge shock to the world when, having boarded an aircraft in England on 15 December 1944, he disappeared into oblivion. He had been on his way to Paris to conclude arrangements with his band for the Christmas Day concert for Allied troops, but he never reached his destination. The true reason for his disappearance remains unknown to this day, although there has been much speculation as to what happened to the famous performer.

It was not unusual during the 1930s and 1940s for aircraft to vanish inexplicably. Such losses were not confined to the Bermuda Triangle but occurred all over the world. While no one could be sure of the reasons for these disappearances, the most probable explanation was that it was mechanical failure because of the fledgling nature of the aviation industry at that time.

Aside from this possibility, two main theories (one from each opposing side of the war) have been put forward to explain what happened to Miller. The German tabloid newspaper *Bild* claimed that Miller had died from a cardiac arrest while in the company of a prostitute. It was suggested that these facts had been covered up by the British and Americans in order to protect the troops' morale. No evidence has ever come to light to support this claim and the Allies dismissed it as mere propaganda.

The Allies maintained that Miller's light aircraft, a Norseman UC-64, had encountered bad weather which had caused it to ditch in the English Channel. It is certainly true that Miller's flight had been delayed for several days by stormy conditions, so there might be some truth behind this theory.

Recently, however, fresh evidence has come to light that may suggest a completely different explanation and might, indeed, reveal elements of a cover-up on the part of the Allies. This new information is contained in the logbook of an RAF navigator, Fred Shaw, and may hold the key to the disappearance. In fact, the revelations within its pages have been described by the Ministry of Defence as 'the most likely solution to the mystery'.

During the war, Shaw carried out bombing raids in an Avro Lancaster, and his records show that, on the day in question, his bomber had been recalled from a raid over Germany due to bad weather. It was usual in these cases for bombers to jettison their load over the sea as a precaution before landing. For this purpose there were specially marked jettison areas which all aircraft were advised to avoid.

It is entirely possible that either Miller's aircraft strayed into this no-go zone, or else the bomber dropped its load outside the defined boundaries. Whatever the case, the bomber reported seeing a small aircraft hit the water after being thrown off track by the bombs.

Whether or not these facts were known to the Allied command at the time is another mystery in itself. It is unlikely, however, that they would have run the risk of damaging public morale during the war. Sixty years later, the truth of the matter may finally be coming to light.

CHAPTER 2

LOST WORLDS AND MYSTERIOUS MONUMENTS

Throughout history, cities and states have sprung up all over the world, achieved their age of greatness and then subsided back into the dust. Some of these lost worlds leave written evidence of their great achievements encrypted in a forgotten language, such as the Egyptian hieroglyph or the Mayan codex. Others may leave behind little more than a puzzling legacy of monuments. They were built to immortalize a set of beliefs, and the scale of their construction shows the effort and dedication that went into their making. Some of these ancient edifices are enigmas, raising more questions than they answer. Why were they built and how?

THE DOGON

The people of the Dogon tribe, in Mali, West Africa, live in small villages miles from anywhere. The nearest civilization is the distant city of Timbuktu. Despite their apparent geographical and cultural isolation, this remote tribe have been in possession of astronomical knowledge that, although now overtaken, was for hundreds of years far in advance of Western understanding.

The first Western scientists to make contact with the Dogon were a pair of French anthropologists – Dr Marcel Griaule and Dr Germaine Dieterlen – who reached the tribe in 1931. Astonished by what they found there, they remained in Mali to research this people for more than thirty years. During this time, they gained access to the Dogon's religious and cultural traditions, and eventually came to earn their trust.

The secret tribal lore of the Dogon revealed that they possessed some fascinating information. Long before Galileo made his revolutionary discoveries in Europe, the Dogon seem to have had knowledge of the rings of Saturn. They were also aware of the existence of the four major moons of Jupiter and knew that the Earth is a planet, and that all planets orbit the Sun.

The tribe also had an extensive understanding of the Sirius binary star system, which was unknown to the West until 1862, when it was spotted from the world's most powerful telescope. The Dogon were fully aware that Sirius actually comprises two stars, Sirius A and Sirius B, which orbit each other in a 50-year cycle with the result that, for a large part of this cycle, only one of the two stars is ever visible.

Sirius A – a bright star that we refer to as the Dog Star – was to the Dogon the most important star in the sky, as they believed that it was here that life originated. Sirius B – which we have discovered is 100,000 times less visible than its twin, and which we class as a 'White Dwarf' star – was known to the Dogon as the second star of this system and described by them as 'the heaviest star'.

Such ideas are relatively recent in modern astronomy yet the Dogon were aware of this information long before instruments such as telescopes were invented. The mystery deepens still further when we consider the tribe's own explanation of how they acquired their detailed astronomical knowledge. According to tribal lore, they were given this information by a race of god-like extra-terrestrials, the Nommo, who originated from the Sirius star system.

Dogon legend tells how the Nommo arrived on a type of spaceship, accompanied by fire and thunder. These aliens were terrifying in their appearance, being fish-like and bearing similarities to the amphibious gods of some other ancient religions such as the Egyptian Isis and the Babylonian Oannes. According to tribal lore, these aquatic beings released huge quantities of water on to the Earth in which to live.

The Dogon referred to Sirius B as 'the Nommo star', and also spoke of a mystical third star, Sirius C, which, to date, has not been recognized by modern science. The tribe called this star the 'Sun of Women', and predicted that it would re-appear in the sky when the Nommo choose to reveal themselves to Earth once again.

The Dogon, therefore, have their own explanation as to how they acquired their remarkable knowledge. But what does the wider world think? Three main theories have been put forward to explain the mystery, and all have their proponents and detractors.

Firstly, it has been suggested that the Dogon may

Sirius A, the brightest star in the night sky.

have learned about Sirius through an undocumented contact with the outside world. However, this argument would seem to be invalidated by the fact that the tribe's knowledge of Sirius was documented on cuneiform tablets many years before modern science even became aware of the star system.

Secondly, it is possible that one of the great ancient civilizations, such as Egypt or Persia, was itself in possession of this astronomical knowledge and had passed it on to a member of the Dogon, perhaps a wandering tribal nomad. This theory seems unlikely, however, since by nature the Dogon people choose to live a life of isolation away from the rest of the world.

The third possible explanation is that perhaps an ancient visionary priest or psychic prophesied this information to the tribe and it became woven into Dogon mythology. However, this seems almost as remarkable an idea as the tribe's own explanation. It seems that perhaps it is the Dogon's own account that we should, after all, take as being the correct one. After all, these people have been proved right on numerous counts already. The fact of their isolation and ignorance of the western world's wider theories pertaining to alien beings lends their explanation further credence. How else could they give a description of an extra-terrestrial unless they had actually encountered one?

The mystery remains, but what seems likely is that supposedly 'primitive' tribes such as the Dogon were, in fact, a lot more advanced than was thought possible.

A Dogon Nommo figure. According to the Dogon, Sirius B was the Nommo star and they had travelled to Earth on a spaceship in the distant past.

A group of Dogon wearing traditional masks, Mali.

CIUDAD BLANCA

Hidden somewhere in the vast, impenetrable jungle of the Central American coast is the legendary 'Ciudad Blanca', or 'White City'. The city is said to have contained incredible wealth and yet was abandoned hundreds of years ago for unknown reasons. Although a number of international expeditions have endeavoured to uncover its secret location and sophisticated satellite technology has been used, the density of the jungle spanning Nicaragua and Honduras is so great that, to date, the task has been impossible.

The first recorded mention of the 'Ciudad Blanca' dates back to 1526, when it was referred to by Hernando Cortes – the Spanish conqueror of Mexico – by the twin names of Xucutaco and Hueitapalan. It is unsurprising that the Spanish were interested in the city as it was said that its riches rivalled those of Tenochtitlan, the wealthy Aztec capital. Inspired by such a notion, Cortes sent many of his followers in search of the lost kingdom, but the treacherous nature of the Mosquito Coast prevented the Conquistadors from finding it and they soon abandoned their search.

It is thought however that, even by the time of the Conquistadors, the 'Ciudad Blanca' was in decline. At that time the area was inhabited by the Pech people, who are believed to have originated from South America. Many skirmishes are recorded as having taken place between the Pech and the Spanish, as well as with the neighbouring tribes.

So what happened to this city, and how did it come to be abandoned? One possible theory is that it may

A fantastical imagining of the 'Ciudad Blanca', by a 20th-century American artist. The idea of a lost city hidden deep in the jungle has fascinated people for centuries.

just have exceeded its natural limits of expansion and was thus abandoned. Or perhaps, already shrinking, it was ultimately unable to survive the arrival of the Conquistadors on the continent, since the Spanish invaders altered the balance of an entire way of life and had a damaging effect on many of the formerly advanced and prosperous civilizations of Meso-America.

The speed at which the jungle of the Mosquito Coast could devour an empty city is remarkable, especially as, prior to the arrival of the Spanish, it had been an incredibly populous area of the world. The 'Ciudad Blanca' is only one of the many undiscovered cities that are hidden in Central America, but for modern Honduras it will be a national and cultural treasure should it ever be recovered.

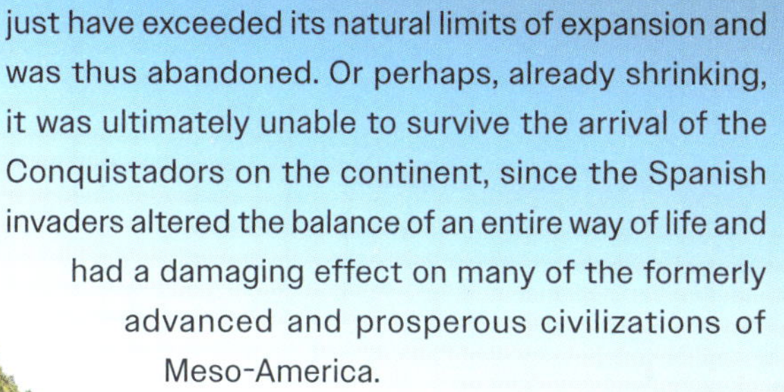

Legends of the 'Ciudad Blanca', a city filled with untold wealth, located somewhere in the Central American jungle, date back to the first Conquistadors.

THE ANASAZI

Little known today, the Anasazi civilization existed for almost one thousand years in the area of the USA now called Arizona and New Mexico. At their cultural peak, in around AD1050, the Anasazi were a thriving community, who built huge structures in which to live. Palaces, some containing up to 500 rooms, were cut into the cliffs and many displayed a considerable complexity of construction. However, by the middle of the 12th century, the society had collapsed and its population had scattered. By AD1300 the tribe had disappeared altogether. The reasons why are unknown to this day.

Early explorers and relic collectors were amazed by what they found of this tribe, uncovering a remarkable abundance of abandoned pottery and artefacts. Initially, the discoveries were credited to the distant Aztecs as it was believed that the indigenous people living in this region would be incapable of constructing such an organized community. Only later did it become apparent that another civilization altogether may have been responsible for them.

The ruins of Chaco Canyon. The Anasazi inhabitants suddenly abandoned the area around 1300 – the reasons are still debated today.

Dwellings were carved into the rock at Bandelier National Monument, an Anasazi site in New Mexico dating back to the 12th century.

The greatest development of structures built by the Anasazi was discovered at Chaco Canyon, New Mexico, and was believed to have been the hub of a community of outlying farms and settlements. Several huge palaces were located here and it is thought that trading, spiritual ceremonies and astronomy were all practised in this central area. Is it conceivable that such a sophisticated community could just vanish?

It has not been unknown over the course of history for civilizations to decline or disappear. Some peoples – such as the residents of Pompeii or the Minoans of Crete – are known to have been wiped out as a result of natural disaster, but the fate of other civilizations remains a cause for speculation. What we do know is that there are numerous factors that could bring about the demise of a civilized society, such as drought, famine or war. At some sites, such as those where burned dwellings have been found, the sad fate of the inhabitants is all too apparent.

The rise and fall of some cities or states has been well documented over time, giving us the opportunity to learn from the mistakes and misfortunes of the past. It is true to say that, at any time, our hold on the status quo is only ever a precarious one, and if we can avoid repeating some of the errors made by our forebears, perhaps we can really be said to have made progress.

Examples of Anasazi pottery. Left: a glazeware bowl with a serpent design from Pecos Pueblo, New Mexico. Right: a pitcher with geometric designs found in Mancos Canyon, Colorado.

THE MOCHE

The Moche people formed the first great civilization of Peru, preceding both the Chimu and the Incas. Although it is known that the Moche lived for about 1,000 years – from around 100BC until about AD900 – their origins are uncertain. Were they indigenous South American people, or was there any truth in local legends that spoke of the tribe arriving by raft, under the leadership of a heroic figure known as 'Naymlpa'?

Equally mysterious is why the Moche culture ultimately faded from the continent. One theory is that it might have been as a result of war, as surviving cultural treasures, such as art and pottery, dating from the latter part of their era seem to reflect a growing preoccupation with militarism.

The Moche were a particularly progressive people for their time, especially in the fields of architecture and engineering. Their vast and durable buildings – some of which are still standing today – were constructed out of adobe bricks, which were made from mud and then baked in the sun. Amazingly, some of these buildings are estimated to contain as many as 100 million bricks.

One of their notable achievements was the building of Chan Chan, the largest pre-Columbian city in America, and this, like all their cities, served a largely religious function. Most of the buildings and pyramids were used

A golden headdress ornament from the Moche culture c. AD200–600.

for the purposes of worship and astronomy. Two of the largest surviving pyramids are known as 'Huacas del Sol y de la Luna', or 'Temples of the Sun and the Moon'. The Moche were not the only ancient culture to display a religious preoccupation with the stars, as many of these early civilizations found great meaning in the motion of the heavens.

Another sign of the Moche's sophistication can be found in their unparalleled systems of irrigation, which are used to this day by local farmers. The Moche created hundreds of miles of irrigation channels and canals, which were filled with water purely by the force of gravity. This system allowed them to gather water from high in the Andes and increase their crop yields. At the height of their success, the region was more highly cultivated and productive than it is today.

Unfortunately, the Moche did not possess a system of writing, so we are limited in what we can learn about and from them. A large part of what we have gleaned is derived from surviving cultural artefacts, many of which were then unfortunately appropriated by those who followed. What this means is that, sadly, many questions about the Moche, these highly advanced progenitors of Peruvian culture, will remain unanswered.

The Huaca de la Luna, or Temple of the Moon, at Chan Chan, capital of the Moche civilization.

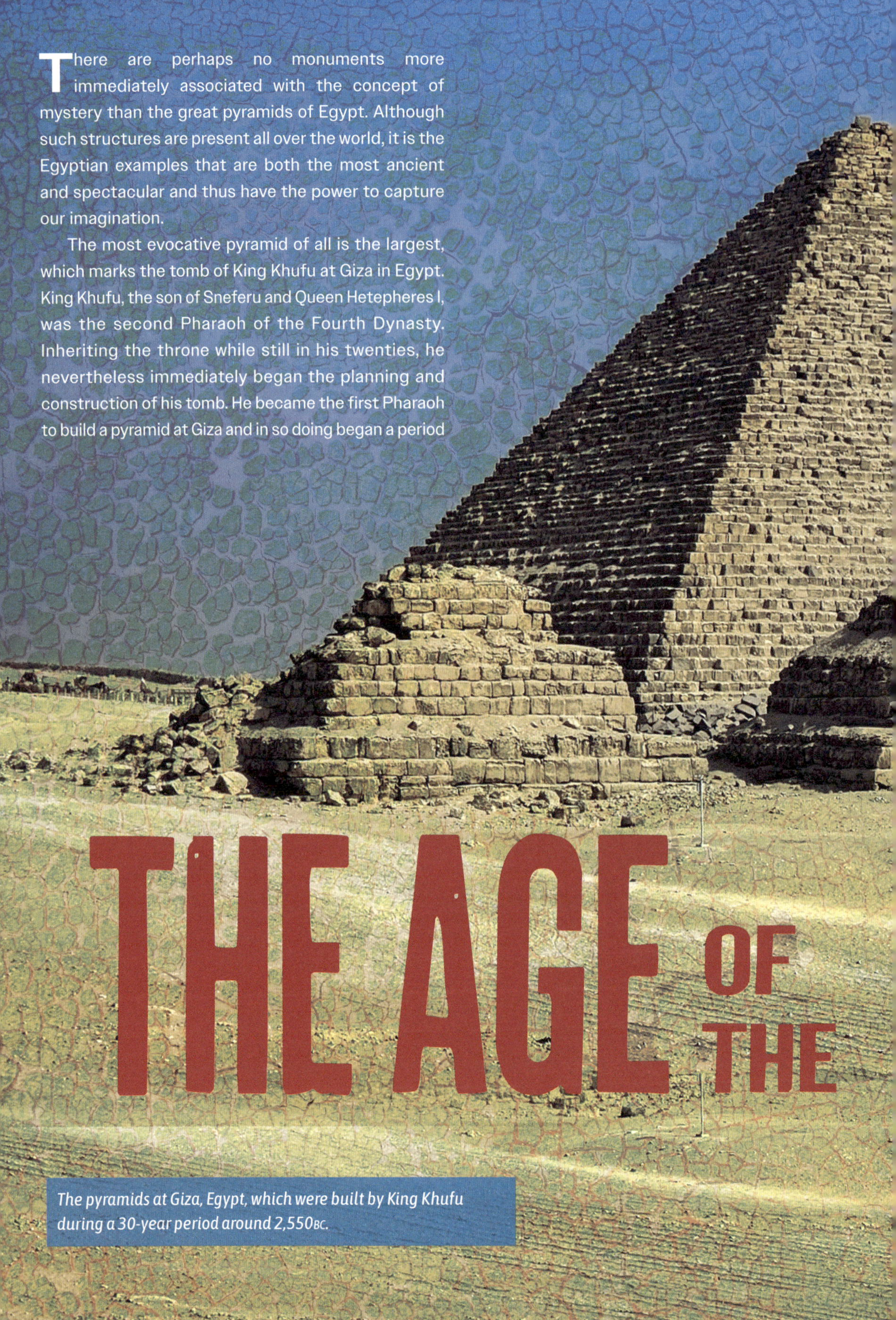

There are perhaps no monuments more immediately associated with the concept of mystery than the great pyramids of Egypt. Although such structures are present all over the world, it is the Egyptian examples that are both the most ancient and spectacular and thus have the power to capture our imagination.

The most evocative pyramid of all is the largest, which marks the tomb of King Khufu at Giza in Egypt. King Khufu, the son of Sneferu and Queen Hetepheres I, was the second Pharaoh of the Fourth Dynasty. Inheriting the throne while still in his twenties, he nevertheless immediately began the planning and construction of his tomb. He became the first Pharaoh to build a pyramid at Giza and in so doing began a period

THE AGE OF THE

The pyramids at Giza, Egypt, which were built by King Khufu during a 30-year period around 2,550BC.

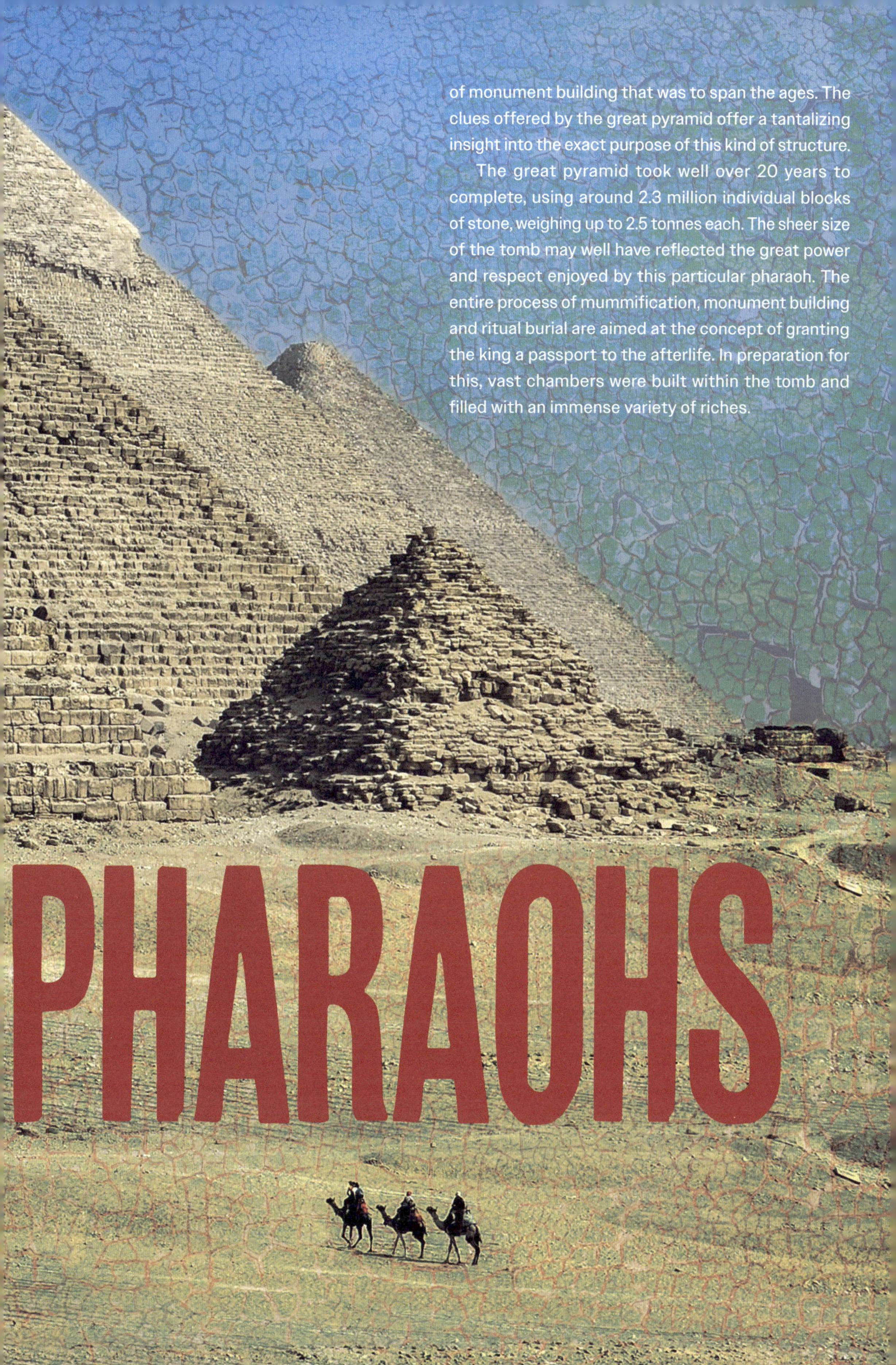

of monument building that was to span the ages. The clues offered by the great pyramid offer a tantalizing insight into the exact purpose of this kind of structure.

The great pyramid took well over 20 years to complete, using around 2.3 million individual blocks of stone, weighing up to 2.5 tonnes each. The sheer size of the tomb may well have reflected the great power and respect enjoyed by this particular pharaoh. The entire process of mummification, monument building and ritual burial are aimed at the concept of granting the king a passport to the afterlife. In preparation for this, vast chambers were built within the tomb and filled with an immense variety of riches.

PHARAOHS

The doorways at the temple of Amun-Ra in Karnak have been carefully aligned to coincide with the setting sun at the spring and winter solstices.

On further examining this pyramid, a number of factors have led many to suspect that there may be some hidden meaning contained within the structure. First, Khufu's personal burial chamber is larger than that of any other pyramid in the world and its construction is of the highest standard. In fact it is so intricate that it contains a small shaft, running all the way from the burial chamber up to the sky in a completely straight line.

The precision of the line is such that some Egyptologists believe it may have been intended as a conduit for the Ka, or spirit of the Pharaoh. It has also been suggested that the line of the shaft from the burial chamber would have aligned with the constellation of Orion at the time of the king's burial and, furthermore, that this pyramid and the two others built at Giza may actually form a representation on Earth of this particular constellation. Support for this theory is provided by the fact that Orion had particular importance for the Egyptians in terms of the afterlife.

There has also been much discussion about the supposed mathematical perfection of the pyramid's dimensions and position. Considering the religious importance of these factors to the Egyptians, these points may be worth considering. Each face of the pyramid is hyper-accurately oriented towards each of the cardinal compass points. The Egyptians used precise geographical North, which is aligned with the spin axis of Earth, rather than magnetic North. This fact demonstrates the Egyptians' advanced understanding of the world and suggests that they were aware that Earth was a sphere that rotated. The position of the great pyramid exactly straddles the 30th parallel latitude, setting it precisely one third

The ancient Egyptian calendar gave a particular astrological meaning to each day and this was reflected in the architecture of the ancient society.

of the way between the North Pole and the Equator. Just as there seems to be a very precise positioning involved in the construction of the pyramid at Giza, so too can a curious alignment be seen in the temple of Amun-Ra at Karnak. Here, doorways to the monument have been built so that they line up exactly along the bearing 26° south of East, to 26° north of West, over the distance of almost 1km (0.6 miles). This coincides exactly with the position of the rising and setting suns on the days of the spring and winter solstices.

Such factors could be coincidental, but taken together they begin to suggest that perhaps the edifices of ancient Egypt contain some greater significance in their structure. The deliberately huge scale of the pyramids would moreover ensure that they defied the ravages of time and thus carry this message into subsequent millennia. Certainly, many Egyptian monuments would seem to demonstrate the importance to this ancient people of certain times of the year, such as the solstices. The Egyptian calendar also followed a kind of cyclical Zodiac that applied a particular cosmic importance to each particular day. This is in its essence very similar to the ideas expressed in astrology today in cultures all over the world.

The pyramids are a potent symbol of mysticism and inspire great curiosity all over the world. Their true meaning and purpose can only be guessed at, and we will probably never know the real answers. Perhaps what is most important, though, is that the pyramids prompt us to ask the right questions, questions about the power and wisdom of the ancients, the nature of civilization and the mysteries of the universe.

BAALBECK

Temples have stood at Baalbeck, in Lebanon, for thousands of years, enduring the rule of numerous civilizations and the worship of many changing gods. They have been altered, but never destroyed, because of their incredible beauty and grandeur. In fact, it is the sheer scale of the temples that has provoked such intrigue and wonder, with archaeologists the world over mystified as to how such impressive structures could have been built so long ago.

Baalbeck was originally a Phoenician settlement which became successively Greek, Roman, Byzantine and then Arab, through conquest. The Greeks occupied the town in 331BC, renaming it Heliopolis (city of the sun). Located on principal trading routes, the city flourished and became a large religious centre.

Wherever structures have survived this long, they have usually been built from stone with the express intention of permanence, and Baalbeck is no exception. In fact, this structure contains the largest cut blocks of stone in the world. Some of these are so large, and quarried from so far away, that experts are mystified not only as to how they were transported to the site, but also how the temple was ever built.

The reason for the inconceivable vastness of the stones was Phoenician tradition, which dictated that the podium for the temple must consist of no more than three layers of stone. When a large extension to the temple site was suggested, the ancient architects realized that they were going to have to work on a scale not previously imagined.

Undeterred by the daunting scale of their task, they commissioned the carving of what were in effect colossal building bricks, hewn from solid rock. Several of these are to be found on the western side of the podium, in the area named the 'Trilithon', after the three largest blocks. These stones are around 20m (66ft) long, 4.5m (15ft) high and 3.6m (12ft) deep, and each is estimated to weigh around 800 tonnes. By way of comparison, these stones are four or five times larger than those at Stonehenge, and approximately 300 times heavier than those used to build the Egyptian pyramids.

Amazingly, the largest of the stones was even heavier than this. At more than 1,000 tonnes, the size and weight of 'the stone of the pregnant woman' would test the greatest cranes in existence in the world today. However, this stone still remains in its quarry, as building work ceased before it ever came to be used.

Aside from the fact that the huge blocks of stone were transported more than 1km (0.6 miles) from their quarry and then raised more than 7m (23ft) into their final positions, there is yet another mystery attached to them. The craftsmanship shown in the construction is of such a high standard, with the stones arranged in such a precise fashion, without the use of mortar, that it is impossible to wedge even the slightest object between them.

The scale of Baalbeck has fired people's imaginations to such an extent that each successive culture to occupy the site has linked the Trilithon with some kind of popular myth, be it giants, biblical figures or even the intervention of extraterrestrials.

The Temple of Baachus in Baalbeck. Baalbeck began life as a Phoenician settlement, before ending up in Greek hands. The remarkable grandeur of its temples has raised questions of just how they were created.

Whatever the explanation for the construction of this vast monument, it looks likely that Baalbeck will continue to draw countless visitors to the site in the future.

No doubt these people, like thousands before them, will marvel at the beauty of this remarkable ancient monument, that suggests so much about the possibilities of human achievement.

The Megalithic tombs of Newgrange, in Ireland, are more than 5,000 years old, so they pre-date the pyramids of Egypt, and even the arrival of the Celts in Ireland. As is often the case with such ancient monuments, very little remains today to give a clue as to the greater purpose behind their construction and this fine Stone Age necropolis is a source of speculation and intrigue all over the world.

Located near the banks of the river Boyne, to the east of Slane, the Newgrange tombs are known in the native tongue as Bru Na Boinne. According to pagan lore, Newgrange was the dwelling of Aengus, the powerful god of love. The site is also associated with the mystical race of the goddess Danu, also known as the Tuatha De Dannan. According to local superstition, these nature-loving pagans have left something of their spirit in the landscape and it is thought that Cuchulain, the legendary hero of the Celtic warriors, was conceived at Newgrange.

During the winter solstice, the dawn sun shines down a passage to the burial chamber, highlighting the intricate carvings within.

The Newgrange tomb is said to be the burial place of the high kings of Tara. The ash remains of these rulers would have been contained in large bowls in each of the three recesses of the burial chamber. Although this chamber has been described as cruciform in shape, given the fact that the tomb pre-dates the birth of Christ by around 3,200 years, it is more likely that this layout reflects the clover form that is so prevalent in ancient Irish artworks.

The builders of these tombs demonstrated considerable devotion to their construction. First, they made use of materials that were not readily available – the quartz must have been quarried and transported from the Wicklow Mountains, a considerable distance from Newgrange. Second, the builders were involved in a huge project – it has been estimated that the construction of the monument would have taken a workforce of 300 men more than twenty years to complete.

In common with the people of other ancient cultures, the lives of the Newgrange community would have been closely regulated by the natural rhythms and cycles of the earth, with the summer and winter solstices assuming great importance. At Newgrange, at the winter

NEWGRANGE

solstice, the dawn sun shines through a 'roof-box', down a short, straight passage and into the heart of the burial chamber, illuminating intricate carvings that are believed to represent the sun and the moon.

Intriguingly, similar effects can be found at Stonehenge, in the pyramids of the Maya and Aztec, and in King Khufu's pyramid in Egypt, where a curious shaft of light enters the tomb at the time of the solstice.

It is unclear whether this shaft may have been intended to allow the king's soul to ascend to the heavens.

Did these cultures have a common spiritual identity, or is there simply something innate in human nature that discovered great profundity in the movement of the stars and the cycles of the planet? These ancient farming communities possessed a knowledge and understanding way ahead of their time. It is impossible not to marvel at the skill that enabled these people to make the precise calculations necessary in order to align the passages of the tombs with the light thrown out by the stars or the sun.

The Newgrange tombs in Ireland are the final resting sites of the high kings of Tara.

STONEHENGE

The towering, mysterious circle of rocks that rises out of Salisbury Plain has inspired awe in millions of people over the ages. But the reason for its existence baffles archaeologists to this day. Various theories suggest a ritual site, an astronomical observatory, or a focus for some mystical form of 'earth energy'.

In piecing together the complex Stonehenge jigsaw, we can at least be confident of some basic facts. Using radiocarbon measurements, scientists have dated the earliest work on Salisbury Plain to around 3,100BC. At this time the site was far more primitive, comprising a circular 97.5m (320ft) diameter ditch, a single entrance and a central wooden 'temple' or sanctuary. Around the edge of the ditch were 56 holes, each containing cremated human remains. On the summer and winter solstices the whole structure aligned with rising and setting points of the moon. By 2,500BC, the wooden sanctuary had been replaced with two circles of the famous bluestones that had been transported 390km (242 miles) from the Preseli mountains of south-west Wales. An entrance avenue of

The mammoth bluestones used to construct Stonehenge were transported almost 400km from the Preseli mountains of south-west Wales to Salisbury Plain.

A painting of Stonehenge by the early-19th-century artist John Constable. The mysteries of Stonehenge have fascinated people for millennia.

parallel ditches which aligned to the midsummer sunrise was added, together with outlying single megaliths such as the Heel Stone, Slaughter Stone and Station Stones. However, the bluestones were pulled down within a century and recycled for a new design. The new Stonehenge had a very different emphasis. At its centre was the Altar Stone (now fallen), a large sandstone shipped from the Cleddau Estuary in Pembrokeshire. Over the next 500 years, some of the re-used bluestones were raised around it in a horseshoe shape. Beyond these were placed five massive sarsen trilithons (two uprights bearing a horizontal), a ring of bluestone pillars and an outer ring of sarsen uprights linked by lintels. The bus-sized sarsen blocks are by far Stonehenge's largest, typically weighing 30 tons and at least one as much as 50 tons. Most are thought to have been transported from the chalklands of Marlborough Downs, some 32km (20 miles) west.

According to some estimates these three building phases must together have required more than thirty million hours of labour. For Stone Age people to allocate this amount of time – even over two millenia – seems extraordinary. It suggests a level of co-operation far above what we might expect; a society in which Stonehenge labourers would have had to be fed, watered and sheltered in order to build a seemingly useless monument. How did they do it? More importantly, why did they do it?

The how is comparatively easy to fathom. Many of north-west Europe's neolithic monument builders used large quantities of stone transported from a great distance. The architects of Newgrange in the Irish Midlands, which predates the Stonehenge megaliths by at least 500 years, brought quartz and granodiorite from sites 48km (30 miles) away. It seems likely that Stonehenge's bluestones were brought to Salisbury Plain by a combination of raft-borne river, sea and overland transport. Once the raw materials arrived, the construction of the circle itself would have required a phenomenal amount of manpower, relying on a levering system of wood and rope.

Manpower aside, the thorny question of quite why it was necessary to lug the bluestones 390km (242 miles) is far from clear. A study led by Geoff Wainwright and

Timothy Darvill in 2004 suggests that the dolerite crags of the Preseli mountains would have held particular appeal. The stone is naturally fractured into 'ready-made' pillars, so they just needed to be levered off for removal. The stones themselves – strong, durable, and speckled with white feldspar – may have been invested with a symbolic, mythical power.

Which brings us back to the key question, what was Stonehenge for? It may well have had different functions at different times. But the prevailing archaeological view is that Stonehenge was a ritual and burial site, linked to astronomical observations. It was almost certainly not used to predict the agricultural crop cycle. In England the summer solstice occurs long after the start of the growing season and the winter solstice misses the harvest by a good three months.

In 2005, tests on some neolithic pig bones showed that large numbers were slaughtered in the months of December or January. This lends weight to the idea that a winter solstice festival was held at Stonehenge. It also seems to have been an important burial site. Around the standing stones are a large number of burial mounds, and in 2002 an archer's grave was discovered that contained more than 100 precious items such as gold earrings, copper knives and pottery. Tests have shown that the deceased – dubbed the 'King of Stonehenge' – was born in the Alps around 2,300BC. This is the richest known burial of the age anywhere in Europe, and the implication is that the 'King' was a settler who played a key role in constructing the monument.

The link between Stonehenge and the ancient Druid religion has taken a battering in recent years. Experts believe this connection was always tenuous (based as it was on the observations of Julius Caesar) and it is now clear that the heyday of the Druids came a thousand years after work on Stonehenge ended. However, we cannot be certain how early the Druid traditions came into existence, so a link cannot be ruled out.

The idea that Stonehenge was used as a celestial calendar is simple to prove. If you stand in the centre of the circle at 5am on a clear Midsummer's Day you can see the sun rise precisely in line with the Heel Stone, 37m (121ft) beyond the ring. This is the most obvious and impressive of the circle's mysterious alignments. During the 1950s and 60s a further 23 alignments were recorded by Oxford University engineer Alexander Thom and the astronomer Gerald Hawkins. Hawkins speculated that Stonehenge was used to predict eclipses, although critics now say his methodology was flawed and that he overestimated the number of alignments. What is clear is that the ancient architects of Stonehenge possessed a level of mathematical and engineering sophistication that defies explanation, knowledge that appears to have pre-dated both the Egyptian and Mesopotamian cultures. How can we explain that 2,000 years before Euclid's Pythagorean 'breakthrough', and more than 3,000 years before Arya Bhata 'discovered' the value of Pi, neolithic Britons were using these concepts to construct Stonehenge?

Putting aside questions of science, another theory

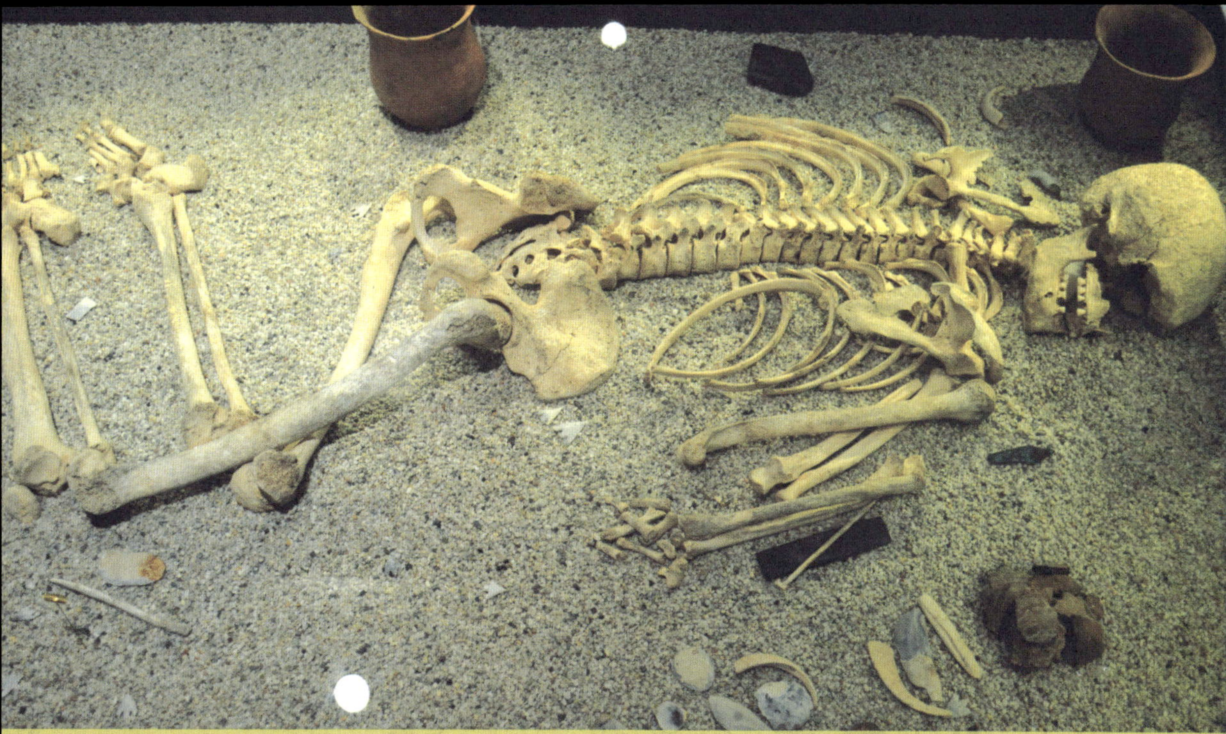

The so-called 'King of Stonehenge', also known as the Amesbury Archer, was found at a nearby burial mound in 2002 with a rich array of artefacts surrounding the body.

behind the existence of Stonehenge is that it focused some intangible 'earth energy', a natural force field that could be tapped by those in the know. Hard evidence for this theory is lacking, although footage of UFOs in the skies above the circle in October 1977 has never been properly explained. All we can say for certain is that Stonehenge seems to be in a significant place: it stands on a known 35km (22-mile) ley line, which also bisects three earthworks and three tumuli (burial grounds).

Maybe the greatest barrier to solving the mystery of Stonehenge lies in our own prejudices. Today we live a hectic urban lifestyle that isolates us from the subtle rhythms of nature observed by neolithic societies. Perhaps we are concentrating too much on scientific knowledge, and our problem in unravelling the mystery of the mammoth stones is that we have started in the wrong place.

ATLANTIS

When it comes to discussing the mystery of Atlantis, there are two opposing views. One view holds that it was a great civilization from long ago, known and discussed among the ancients. The other insists it is a long-standing fabrication, a fictional island that represents a lost Eden.

The most significant account of Atlantis is by the ancient philosopher Plato (427–347BC) in two stories called Critias and Tinnaeus. The sceptics claim that the entire account is a metaphor, and that Plato is using Atlantis to illustrate the disastrous fate of corrupt regimes. Yet significantly Plato says more than once that the stories he recites are true. Nowhere else in his work does he claim allegorical events to be real.

So just what does Plato say about this utopian Atlantis? Well, it was big – larger than Asia and Libya combined. Its people were virtuous, its soldiers skilful, its kings wise. There were fertile plains backed by picturesque mountains, hot and cold springs, horse racing and elephants. A central temple was adorned with golden statues. A system of deep-water canals enabled shipping to enter the city. Likewise, a man-made irrigation system kept crops green and abundant.

Plato was the first to mention the submerged civilization of Atlantis.

This 17th-century woodcut shows the supposed location of Atlantis.

Curiously, Plato makes much of a precious metal called orichalcum that was mined in Atlantis and was a familiar decoration of the buildings there. It was, he says, second only to gold in value. But even by Plato's time, this prized commodity had vanished. No one knows precisely what type of metal orichalcum is, although it is mentioned years later by the Roman commentator Josephus in relation to Solomon's Temple. But here too, evidence is scarce, and there is little archaeological data to confirm the materials used in that great temple. Whatever the physical properties of orichalcum, it seems certain that it was of great value to ancient cultures, and that Atlantis was rich in it.

According to Plato, Atlantis was an island once ruled by Poseidon, god of the sea. Poseidon fell in love with a native of Atlantis and she bore him five sets of twins. Admittedly, this part of his story does not seem to be anchored in reality, and the date is implausible. Plato dates the era of Atlantis to 9,000 years before his own day. Today, we have no knowledge of sophisticated civilizations existing so early in human history. It would have been a shining jewel in a Stone Age world.

But if Atlantis did exist, it was doomed to destruction. Plato's account tells how, within a single day and night, a natural disaster eradicated the entire civilization. This is entirely credible, since we know how powerful and ruthless nature can be. The island apparently disappeared into the depths of the sea, leaving only a shoal of mud that barred shipping from the area thereafter. Presumably an earthquake was to blame for the wholesale destruction, which would have extinguished the lives of countless thousands.

Initially it might sound like Plato was recycling some favourite myths that have cropped up down the ages. Atlantis bears some resemblance to a Garden of Eden, while its destruction might be likened to a great flood similar to the one in the Bible and in numerous other beliefs. But why then did Plato go into such historical detail about the civilization and the metal they mined? What if Atlantis was simply the ancient name for another culture that had been wiped out, one that we have evidence of today?

For a long time it seemed as if Plato must have been referring to the Minoan civilization on Crete. This was named only relatively recently by an archaeologist, and no one knows what Plato's contemporaries would

The Minoan Palace of Knossos at Crete. One more recent theory is that the civilization was in fact that of the Minoan people.

have called it. The Minoans had glorious palaces, paved roads and running water. A colossal volcanic eruption on the island of Thera 100km (62 miles) away from Crete caused wholesale destruction in the region, but it did not obliterate the Minoans immediately. Archaeological evidence indicates they survived the tsunamis and the noxious sulphur clouds that must have followed the volcanic explosion, but fared poorly in the face of the ensuing climate change. By 1450BC the Minoan civilization had burnt out, succumbing either to starvation, insurrection or invaders.

Perhaps it was to the Minoans that Plato was referring? However, he confidently dates Atlantis to an era far earlier than that of the Minoan civilization on Crete. It leads one to speculate where the Minoans might have lived before migrating to the island.

Other sites for Atlantis have been put forward at various times throughout history, and these have been as far flung as Spain, South America, the Caribbean, Cyprus and the South China Seas. The evidence for Spain has been supported by satellite photographs, which appear to show concentric circles like those described by Plato. Although the size of the circles does not exactly match the philospher's description, this might be accounted for by a mistake in translating his unit of measurement, the stade, to present day measurements. The proposed site lies in salt marshes near Cadiz.

Ancient writings contain accounts of attacks on Egypt and the eastern Mediterranean by 'the Sea People'. One theory is that the Sea People, the Atlanteans and the Iron Age residents of southern Spain, known as the Tartessos, were one and the same people.

Tiahuanaco in the Bolivian Andes of South America has been earmarked as a possible Atlantis. Satellite photography has revealed it boasted hundreds of miles of inland canals. The residents are believed to have been of the Aymara tribe, a pre-Inca civilization. Such an investment in waterways implies they were a

An artist's conception of the ruins of Atlantis. Despite the long-held fascination with the city, no one has yet been able to locate it.

seafaring race who probably traded with Europeans and Africans. Generally, Tiahuanaco is thought to have dated from the middle of the first millennium (c. AD500) but one researcher, Arthur Broznansky, was certain it was significantly older.

Elusive in place and time, it seems impossible, even using modern technology, to pin down Atlantis to one geographical location.

Nevertheless, many beliefs have sprung from the possible existence of Atlantis. Many people believed it to be the single root of all civilization. The odd coincidences of ancient history, like the way pyramids were built on both sides of the Atlantic and that various races chose to write in hieroglyphics, might have been explained by the existence of the great Atlantis. But there is no evidence of a linking civilization, and science has largely dismissed such claims. The Nazis believed the Atlanteans were a superior race and the ancestors of the Aryans, those favoured by the unsavoury fanatics for peopling the earth. Hitler's henchman Heinrich Himmler was particularly taken with the theory and invested much in a fruitless search.

There have even been claims that the Atlanteans were in fact highly advanced aliens. These assertions have proved popular, but evidence hard to come by. Edgar Cayce, the famous American psychic and healer, maintained that Atlantean existence focused on a giant crystal. This was used not only for healing but in a psychic sense for communication and teleportation. Disaster struck when the crystal exploded. Although they seem bizarre, Cayce's theories are backed by thousands of people today. He remains the inspiration behind the Association for Research and Enlightenment, based in America but present in 60 different countries.

If the mystery of Atlantis has retained its grip on human imagination for so long, it is because it remains a powerful symbol of the nature of human civilization, reminding us that however wealthy and powerful nations become, the forces of time and nature will eventually overcome them.

YONAGUNI

In 1985, a discovery was made in Japan that still baffles the scientific community today. A Japanese dive tour operator, Kihachiro Aratake, strayed from his regular area into the waters off Yonaguni Island, near Okinawa. About 30m (98ft) beneath the surface, he found a strange formation which, on further examination, appeared to be a man-made pyramid.

Ever since this date, the Yonaguni finding has been a source of immense controversy. Experts are unable to agree upon whether it is actually a man-made structure at all, or simply a remarkable natural formation. If it can be confirmed to be man-made, it will undoubtedly revolutionize the way in which the history of our own species is viewed.

Scientists agree that this area of coastline became submerged by the rising oceans at least 10,000 years ago. Following the end of the last Ice Age, there was a huge global thaw that altered the world immeasurably and, over time, sea levels are believed to have risen by up to 30m (98ft). This means that any civilization in place at that time would have been destroyed, engulfed by

A diver explores the Yonaguni monument, a pyramid-like structure lying 30m (98ft) beneath the waves.

Kihachiro Aratake, the diver who discovered the Yonaguni monument.

the rising waters, with all traces of it remaining hidden to this day.

Furthermore, it is known that human civilizations have thrived on coastlines for thousands of years, because the sea is not only an excellent source of food, but also facilitates important activities such as trading and transport. Yonaguni would, therefore, have been a likely location for a settlement to arise. Such a civilization would, however, have pre-dated all known cultures by thousands of years, since the oldest known city is believed to be Sumeria in Mesopotamia, which dates back to around 5,000 years ago. To double the accepted timescale of human development is to take a drastic leap. This, however, is not impossible, especially if there is real evidence to support it, as Yonaguni might prove to be.

Perplexing scientists still further is the fact that similarities have been noted between the architecture that appears to exist at Yonaguni and that which can be found above the sea on the coast of Peru.

Yet even the oldest of these Peruvian structures, built by the Moche people, are at the most 2,000 years old, leaving an inexplicable gap of many millennia.

Further controversy has arisen over the actual appearance of the Yonaguni structure. Underwater photographs of the site appear to show the presence of ramps, terraces and steps. While American geologists argue that these are nothing more than natural formations, Japanese scientists have claimed that tool markings can be found along the structure, suggesting that it might have been tampered with.

One person, however, has seemingly taken both sides of the argument, asserting that the site is both natural and man-made. Dr Robert M. Schoch, a geologist who made frequent dives to the site, actually suggested that the majority of the structure was indeed a natural formation, but one that had been chosen and modified by humans, in a process known as 'terra-forming'. The discovery of what appeared to be a small staircase on the site was prime evidence of such modification.

The discovery of structures beneath the sea always generates intrigue and excitement, with people proclaiming that the lost city of Atlantis has been uncovered. However, the location of Yonaguni means that it is unlikely to be Atlantis. Rather, it would seem to have closer parallels to the lost continents of Mu or Lemuria, as both were said to exist in the region of Asia, spanning the Pacific and Indian oceans respectively.

Although the comparatively modern science of tectonics has largely discredited the notion that there were ever 'lost continents', many believe that they did, in fact, exist. Lemuria and Mu are supposed to have been destroyed by immense natural disasters that engulfed the continents. It is not impossible that ancient myths telling of the demise of whole civilizations have become altered and enhanced over time to encompass the destruction of entire continents. In this respect it could actually be possible that the end of the Yonaguni culture could have been mythologized or exaggerated into a story such as that surrounding Lemuria.

In drawing these parallels between Yonaguni and the mythical continents, the experts involved are hoping to

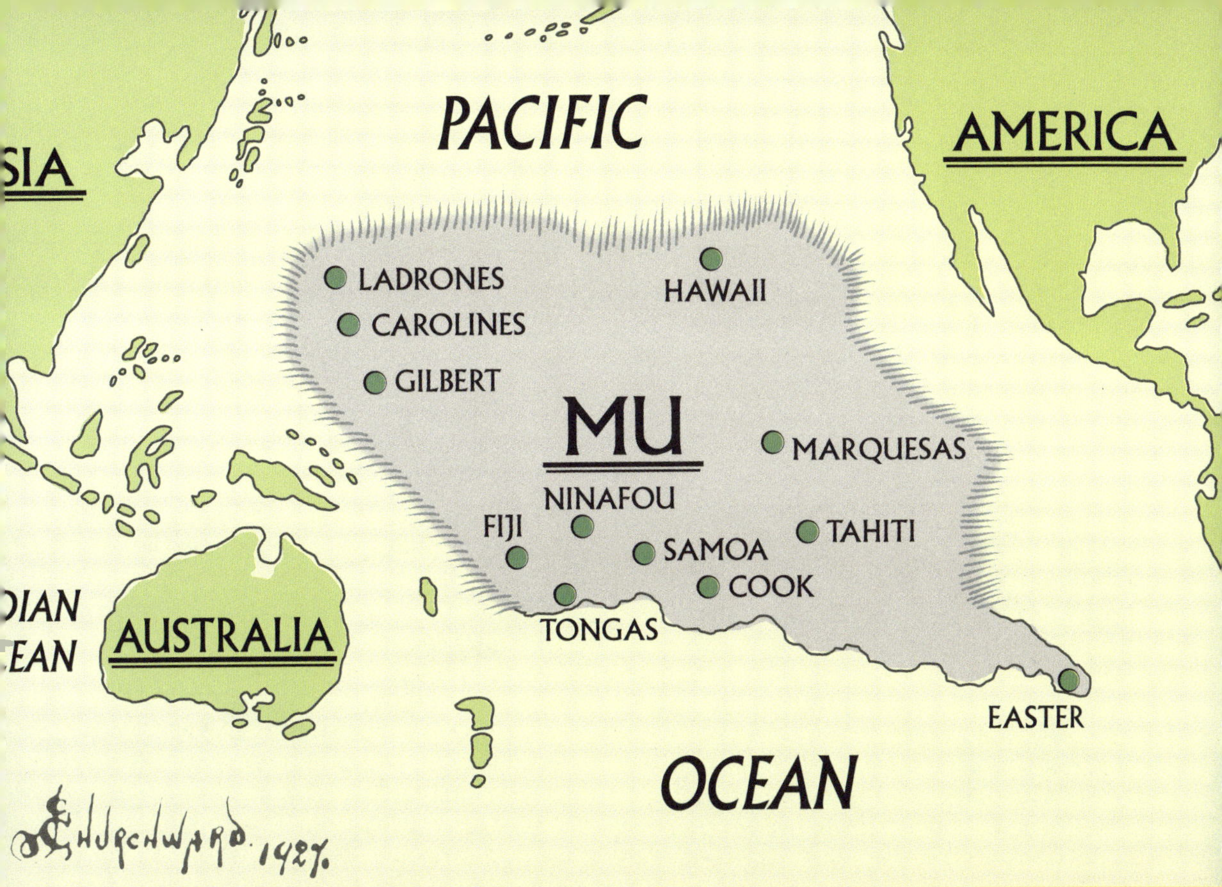

Some have speculated that the Yonaguni monument belonged to the lost continent of Mu.

advance the theory that there is a great lost culture of the Pacific. Tantalizing glimpses of such a culture are offered by the mysterious stone heads of Easter Island or the oral traditions of the Polynesian islands. Apparent similarities between Yonaguni and stone constructions on Hawaii and Tonga suggest a cultural bridge from pre-historic Japan to the coast of South America.

This theory also attempts to explain the similarities between many different cultures of the world, a large number of which shared a belief in astronomy and adopted the pyramid as a favoured type of construction. Some theorists, such as Graham Hancock, believe that this serves as evidence of an ancient seafaring culture that spread its wisdom around the globe. It is certain, however, that further proof will be required before the sceptical world of archaeology accepts such a drastic reinterpretation of man's early history.

Perhaps, if the site around the pyramid is explored further, this evidence might be found after all. Or, if not, it is possible that proof could be located at other formations that have been discovered on the sea-bed close to the Japanese islands of Kerama and Chatan. Now that technology is able to reveal more and more about global changes as a result of the Ice Age, it seems likely that further discoveries of this kind will be made in shallow coastal shelves around the world.

This offers us the exciting prospect of possible answers as to the nature of the origins of human civilization, but as always, each discovery is likely to raise further questions. Why, for example, has the pyramid been so evident in disparate cultures at different times of mankind's history? The answer to this question looks set to remain one of the greatest mysteries of the ancient world.

THE NAZCA

An aerial view of the Nazca lines criss-crossing the Peruvian desert. Could these really be some kind of communication for extraterrestrial visitors?

LINES

Across a 434km² (168 square mile) stretch of Peru's Nazca desert, archaeologists have identified 13,000 lines and pictures etched into the sun-baked surface. That these images were produced by an ancient civilization is beyond doubt. But their purpose is far harder to explain.

The designs were first noticed in the 1920s, as manned flights began to venture into South America. Pilots reported seeing straight lines which ran for miles, traversing mountains and occasionally ending on cliff edges. Geometric shapes included triangles, rectangles, spirals, wavy lines and concentric circles. Animal geoglyphs included birds, whales, a dog and a lizard. Some images were drawn on a truly vast scale: a 305m (1,000ft) pelican, a 285m (935ft) bird with a curiously zig-zag shaped neck and a monkey complete with 100m (328ft) spiral tail.

There were also more surreal pictures – specifically an 'astronaut' figure and a bizarre creature with two colossal hands, one of which had only four digits. Was this, as some have claimed, an attempt to record contact between prehistoric humans and alien beings?

Before considering this and other interpretations of Nazca, it is worth setting out areas of agreement among experts. Firstly, it is obvious that the lines were made by removing the desert's top layer of iron-oxide-coated stones to reveal lighter-coloured soil underneath. Secondly, it is accepted that this must have been a colossal effort, perhaps lasting a thousand years, and that because of the scale of the work the artists could never have seen the full fruits of their labours from the ground. The lines are so unobtrusive that during the last century the pan-American highway was built straight through them without anyone noticing. Thirdly, it seems likely that the patterns were made by ancient Nazca Indians sometime between 400BC–AD600. This estimate is based on radiocarbon analysis of Nazca fire and ceramic debris, although it is not conclusive, since the lines themselves cannot be radiocarbon-dated.

It is possible that an even older civilization did some of the hard work, perhaps evolving from the Paracas culture which blossomed in southern Peru between 1100-200BC. The Paracas people are thought to have constructed the giant El Candelabro geoglyph. Also known as the Tres Cruces or the Trident, this form stretches to more than 120m (394ft) wide. It is situated on a slope overlooking the Bay of Paracas, together with some 50 figures – humans, birds, cats and monkeys – near the Peruvian city of Palpa.

The first academic to make a proper study of Nazca was Paul Kosok, an American who stumbled across the site in the late 1930s while researching prehistoric irrigation systems. He suspected that the lines were linked to astronomical alignments, a theory reinforced when in the late afternoon of the southern hemisphere's winter solstice (22 June) he and his wife witnessed the sun set precisely at the end of one line. Kosok enlisted the help of a German astronomer, Maria Reiche, and together they developed the idea that some Nazca shapes were used as a calendar to help farmers calculate crop planting times. The animals, they believed, represented major constellations. Another American scientist, Gerald Hawkins (see Stonehenge on page 62) used a specialist computer program to calculate the number of significant solar alignments produced by the Nazca lines. He decided that alignments would have to point consistently to a specific celestial event, such as the rising or setting of stars, sun and moon. Neither was it enough merely for some lines to fulfil the criteria. If the astronomical link were to be proved, then it had to account for all the lines.

Hawkins instructed his computer to show how many were aligned on extreme positions of the sun or moon. The answer was 39 out of 136, barely better than would be expected by chance. Worse, only a few of these 39 alignments could be linked to significant solar or lunar positions. Hawkins tried a similar experiment with the stars, inputting a catalogue of their positions dating back to 10,001BC. Again, the alignments were statistically insignificant.

Erich von Daniken courted controversy when he made the claim that the Nazca lines were the markings of an alien spaceport.

In 1968, as Hawkins published his results, the Swiss writer Erich von Daniken inflamed the Nazca debate by claiming that the lines marked out a giant alien spaceport. His book *Chariots of the Gods* essentially argued that it was impossible for ancient people, incapable of flight, to

The El Candelabro geoglyph in southern Peru. It is more than 180m (591ft) tall and was likely created around 200BC.

One of the more bizarre geoglyphs has few recognizable features other than two huge hands, one of which has only four digits.

have produced the drawings themselves and that they must have been taught by visiting aliens.

Critics accused von Daniken of making the facts fit his theory. His cause was not helped by a television investigation into pottery fragments which, he claimed, dated from biblical times and depicted flying saucers. Unfortunately, von Daniken's fragments proved to be of more recent vintage, after television journalists found and interviewed the potter who made them.

As if to rub salt into his wounds, a flamboyant American publisher and adventurer called Jim Woodman set out to prove that Nazca people could, in any case, have known how to fly. Using cloth and rope based on samples found in Indian graves, and reeds cut from Lake Titicaca on the Bolivian border, he constructed a 2,260m^3 hot-air balloon, powered by heat from a bonfire on the ground. Together with the British balloonist Julian Nott, Woodman ascended to a height of 90m (295ft), neatly illustrating that Nazca designers could well have had the technology to fly and monitor progress of their work. This theory may sound far-fetched, but archaeologists have already shown that at least 500 years earlier, Paracas doctors were performing brain surgery through trephination – the removal of skull sections with a cylindrical saw.

Yet even if the ancient inhabitants of South America had the means to make the lines, this still does not explain what they were for. Few archaeological sites have spawned quite so many theories, and in recent years Nazca has been cast as a giant map of subterranean water sources, a focus for earth energies (rather like Stonehenge), a cathedral plan, an athletes' racetrack and even a giant loom on which vast teams of weavers produced cloths or nets. Even harder to grasp is the idea that the Nazca lines are located on a global 'Code Matrix' in which the world's significant ancient sites correlate precisely to the Great Pyramid at Giza. Evidence for this is reportedly found in the geometry of Nazca's layout.

The most likely explanation is that the lines were linked to religious or magical ceremonies. Nazca was an agricultural society skilled in planting, irrigation, harvesting, storage and distribution, but it was also vulnerable to natural disasters and disease. Could the lines have been communal sites for appeasing or worshipping specific gods? Perhaps they served as a gentle reminder of the needs of the Nazca people, and a prompt for regular help from on high. The truth is that, even discounting the role of alien architects, the purpose of the lines remains frustratingly elusive.

THE ARTHUR STONE

The legend of King Arthur is one we are all familiar with, but we are not so sure of the historical facts concerning his life. On 4 July 1998, an archaeologist working at Tintagel Castle in Cornwall unearthed an inscribed chunk of slate. It bore the name Arthnou – an early version of Arthur – re-opening a furious academic controversy about where the 'Once and Future King' of the Britons resided.

The discovery of what became known as 'The Arthur Stone' caused a sensation in archaeological circles. The chief archaeologist of English Heritage, the government-backed body which manages the castle site in North Cornwall, declared it 'the find of a lifetime'. Dr Geoffrey Wainwright added: 'It is remarkable that a stone has been discovered with the name "Arthnou" inscribed on it at Tintagel, a place with which the mythical King Arthur has long been associated.' What so excited Dark Age historians was that the stone emerged from a proven 'sealed context', meaning it had lain undisturbed since at least the 7th century AD.

Professor Christopher Morris holds the Arthur Stone at Tintagel shortly after it had been discovered. This remarkable artifact bears an early form of the name Arthur – 'Arthnou'.

Measuring 20cm x 35cm (8in x 14in), and 1cm (0.4in) in depth, it was originally a plaque of some kind, and bore the Latin words: Pater coli avi ficit artognov – 'Arthnou, father of a descendant of Coll, has had (this) made/built/constructed'.

Quite what he had constructed remains unclear, because the slate had been broken and re-cycled as a 7th-century drain cover. However 'Arthnou' was clearly once a leader of means and stature. In Britain of the Dark Ages, literacy was the preserve of monks and the educated nobility.

Previous excavations at Tintagel had produced fragments of wine and oil pots imported from the Mediterranean, suggesting that the castle was a high-status, secular site, possibly the royal court of a chieftain of Dumnonia (the ancient kingdom of southwest Britain). The slate's significance was that it proved people here were reading and writing Latin, and living a Romanized way of life, 200 years after the Romans left in AD410, which is exactly the period when King Arthur was supposed to have been in power.

In unravelling the mystery of the Arthur Stone, it is important to separate the legendary story of the King from the historical version (such as it is). Few other areas of ancient British history produce quite so much disagreement among scholars and given that there at least nine competing claims for 'ownership' of Arthur – Brittany, Cornwall, Cumbria, Scotland, Somerset, three areas of Wales, Wiltshire, Warwickshire and Yorkshire – it is hard to see a consensus emerging.

What is clear is that Arthurian legend has been much reproduced and embellished over the years. Fantasies such as Malory's 15th-century tome *Le Morte D'Arthur*, Tennyson's *Idylls of the King* and T. H. White's *The Once and Future King* have all contributed to Arthur's legendary status. In these books we learn how Arthur founds his court on the principle of 'might for right', valiantly defending his kingdom against the invading Saxons. He thrives under the counsel of the wizard Merlin but is eventually betrayed by the adultery of his best friend, Sir Lancelot, with his Queen, Guinevere, and dies a hero's death in the 'last battle' against evil forces led by his nephew Mordred. Despite this, according to the old stories, he lies buried in a secret tomb and will return to aid his people in their hour of need.

The Arthur legend is loosely based on the writings of the 12th-century canon Geoffrey of Monmouth, whose *History of the Kings of Britain* was widely read in Europe. Geoffrey's declared aim was to promote patriotism by extolling the glories of the early Britons, but unfortunately the distinction between fact and myth is lost in his work. When Geoffrey wrote of Arthur's birthplace as Tintagel, he was mis-translating an earlier text which used the term 'din-dagol', an old Welsh word meaning 'double-banked hillfort'. He also wrongly believed the Cornovii tribe, supposed ancestors of the King, were based in Cornwall, although they actually controlled what is now the West Midlands. In fact some historians argue that Cornwall has the weakest claim of all to an Arthurian link.

However, just because the written history of sixth and 7th-century Britain is unreliable, this does not mean that traditional folk tales and oral records should be discounted. An oral system worked pretty well for the

Vikings, who relied on it for centuries in matters of law and governance. In Iceland there was even an elected Lawspeaker whose job was to hold the law in his memory and recite a third of it each year, for three years, at the main annual assembly. The problem of course is that oral history is easier to manipulate.

The story of Arthur's quest for the Holy Grail is a case in point. Portraying the king as a defender of Christianity against pagan Britain was nothing more than skilful spin-doctoring by missionary monks keen to claim converts. Just as they built churches on sacred pagan sites, so they adapted traditional stories to suit their religious agenda. Arthur, if he ever existed, was almost certainly a pagan.

And yet the legend of the Holy Grail may be an oral allegory for actual events. It draws heavily on the concept of a freezing wasteland where no crops grow, where famine is rife and plague stalks the countryside. Climatologists now believe that the Arthurian period may have seen just such a scenario, perhaps caused by a mass of debris from comets in the atmosphere which partially blocked light from the sun. Contemporary records from elsewhere in Europe bear this out – the Mediterranean writer Zachariah for instance talks of 'fire from heaven' – and an analysis of oak tree rings suggests growth was severely curtailed between AD539 and 541.

The 12th-century cleric Geoffrey of Monmouth's History of the Kings of Britain *set the stage for the King Arthur legend and described Tintagel as King Arthur's birthplace.*

The ruins of Tintagel dominate the dramatic Cornish coastline. Could this have been the home of the legendary Arthur?

So was there ever a 'real' Arthur figure? Many Dark Age historians now believe that a militarily successful and charismatic leader did emerge in Britain after the fall of the Roman Empire and that his name lived on in folk memory well before any meaningful written accounts. The 9th-century historian Nennius tells us that Arthur was a former Roman General, but offers little by way of explanation. To confuse matters further, it is likely that the name 'Arthnou' (which originally meant 'known as a bear, known to be a bear') was common among the ancient Britons.

Could Arthur's court have been at Tintagel? There are certainly plenty of legends linking the King to Cornwall, among them a stone slab at Slaughterbridge, near Camelford, which is said to mark his grave. Other stories claim his magical sword Excalibur lies at the bottom of either Dozmary Pool on Bodmin Moor, or Loe Pool near Helston, where it was thrown by St Bedivere as Arthur lay dying. The waterfall at St Nectan's Kieve, near Tintagel, is supposedly the place where Arthur baptized his knights before they embarked on their search for the Grail. English Heritage has been careful to play down any clear, evidential link between the Arthur Stone and either the historical or the legendary king. However as Dr Wainwright puts it: 'Tintagel has presented us with evidence of a court of the Arthurian period with buildings, high-status finds and the name of a person, Arthnou. Arthnou was here, that is his name on a piece of stone.'

Shrouded in mystery and yet somehow familiar, the Arthur stone is a unique archaeological find where, as Dr Wainwright put it, 'myth meets history.'

CHAPTER 3

PARANORMAL

Within human society there are groups of people whose remarkable talents and abilities set them apart from the crowd. This is because they are able to break the rules that seem to bind the rest of us – whether these are the laws of physics, such as gravity, or the ability to cross the divide between the worlds of the living and the dead. Various terms are used to describe these people, such as mediums, psychics, telekinetics or healers, and there are innumerable examples of the amazing feats achieved by these people in every civilization and country throughout history.

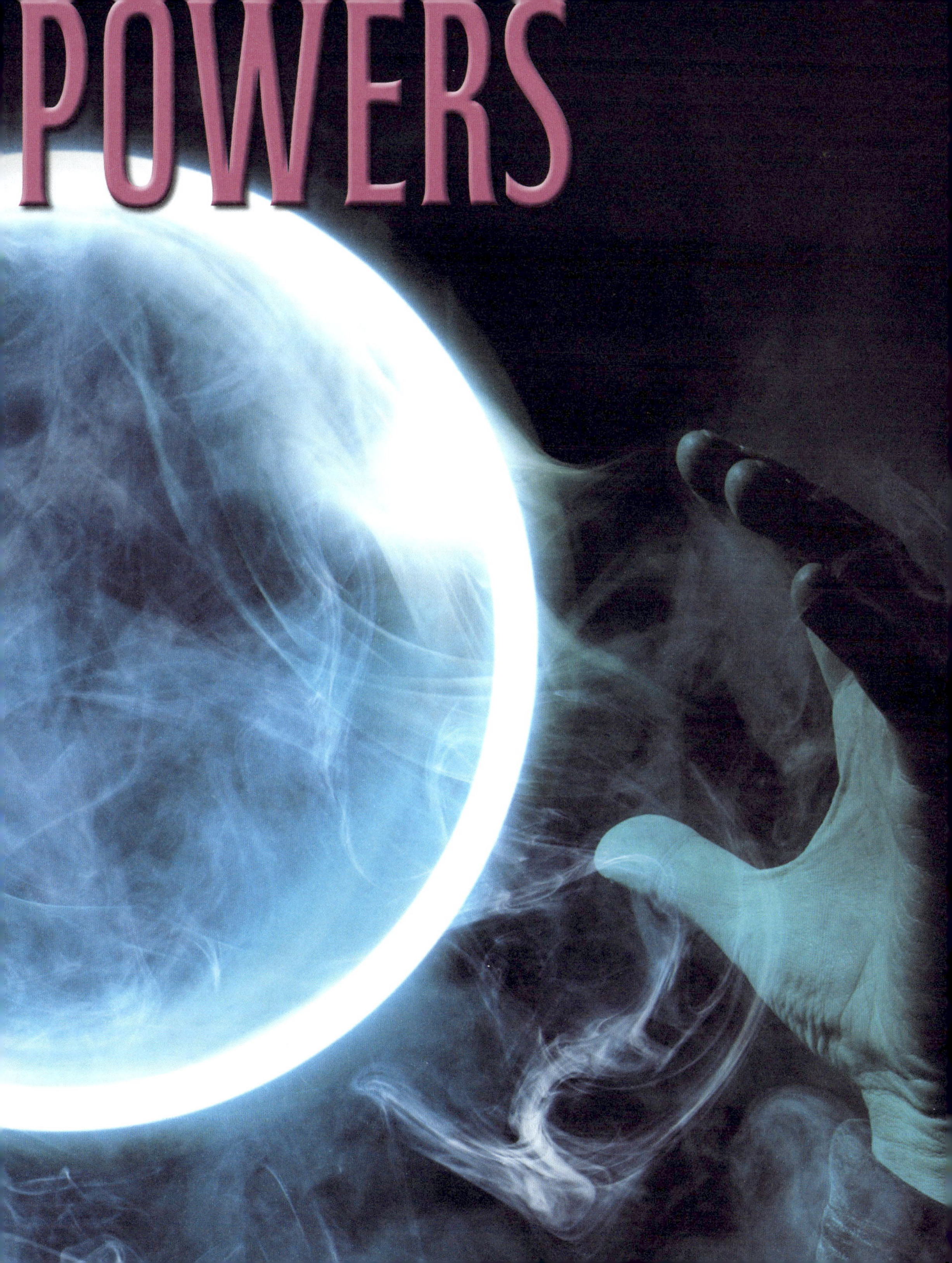
POWERS

EILEEN GARRETT

Eileen Garrett was one of the most respected mediums of the 20th century, who possessed remarkable psychic abilities. In one particular séance, she astounded those present – and made headlines around the country – with her uncannily accurate observations. Garrett is also renowned for the assistance she gave to the scientific community in the investigation and explanation of paranormal powers.

Born in 1893 in Beauparc, County Meath, Ireland, Garrett's early years were troubled, as is often the case among those with psychic abilities. Shortly after she was born both her parents committed suicide, leaving the infant Eileen to be adopted and raised by her aunt and uncle. Her gifts became apparent from a very young age. Not only was she able to see auras of light and energy around living things during her childhood, but she also had a large number of imaginary playmates, who took on a very physical appearance to her.

It seems that at this time Garrett was also visited by visions of the dead. She later described the first of these occasions, in which she observed one of her aunts, who lived some distance away, walking up the pathway towards her house with a baby in her arms. The aunt told her that she had to go away and that

Eileen Garrett possessed astonishing psychic abilities which were present from a young age.

she was taking the infant with her. The following day it was discovered that this aunt had died in childbirth, along with the baby. Such communication with the dead proved to be an increasingly frequent occurrence throughout Garrett's life.

Having contracted tuberculosis as a child, a condition that was to affect her repeatedly for the rest of her days, Garrett moved to the milder climes of England at the age of 15. Before long, she was married to her first husband, Clive, and she bore him four children. Tragically, her three sons all died very young, two of them from meningitis. Her daughter survived, but by this stage the marriage had ended in divorce.

During World War I, Garrett met a young officer through her work at a hospital for wounded soldiers and subsequently remarried. Shortly after he left her to join the fighting at the front, she was visited by a vision of her new husband. Two days later she was informed that he had been killed in action at Ypres.

Amazingly, until this point Garrett had not investigated her remarkable powers to any real extent. However, another period of ill health afforded her the time to consider her unusual abilities and she began to attend séances and table-rapping sessions.

She later recalled that it was at one of these events that she started to feel overwhelmingly drowsy and drifted off into slumber. When she awoke, she discovered that she had actually entered a trance, and that during this state her body had been used by the dead as a means of communicating with living people in the room. Shortly after this she made her first contact with the spirit of Uvali, a 14th-century Arab soldier who was to become her primary contact with the spirit world at future séances.

After a while, Eileen's growing reputation as a psychic brought her to the attention of a well-known psychic investigator, Harry Price. In October 1930, Price arranged for Garrett to be present at a special séance at the National Laboratory of Physical Research. It was hoped that she would be able to contact the spirit of the famous

Harry Price, psychic investigator, arranged to examine Garrett at a séance, at which Arthur Conan Doyle was present.

French firemen holding up a Royal Air Force flag found among the wreckage of the R101 airship.

writer, Sir Arthur Conan Doyle, who had recently died. In preparation, Price arranged for both his secretary and a journalist, Ian D. Coster, to be present to authenticate and document the findings.

It was, therefore, initially disappointing for all concerned when Garrett failed to make contact with Conan Doyle, who had been a spiritualist himself. However, their disappointment soon gave way to astonishment when Garrett proceeded to bring forth the spirit of a Flight Lieutenant H. Carmichael Irwin. It slowly dawned on those present at the séance that this man had been an officer on the R101, Britain's largest airship, which had crashed in France two days earlier, killing 48 of its 54 passengers.

Subsequent news reports of the séance came to the attention of a Mr Charlton, who had been involved in the construction of the airship. Intrigued by what he read, he then asked to see the notes of the séance proceedings. These filled him with amazement, as it transpired that, while in a state of trance, Garrett had produced more than 40 specific pieces of highly technical, confidential information. It would have been impossible, he maintained, for Garrett to have had prior knowledge, or understanding, of such matters.

Charlton was so impressed by these discoveries that he alerted his superiors at the Ministry of Civil Aviation, after which it was decided to hold another séance with Garrett. This time, Major Villiers from the Ministry was in attendance while very specific technical questions were put to Garrett to try to gain further information about the air accident. Detailed answers to these questions were relayed through Garrett, who was able to pinpoint the exact cause of the disaster, even naming the very girder that had failed.

The official court of inquiry examined all of the evidence produced by Garrett during the séance and concluded that it was genuine. Experts declared that it would not have been possible for her to be aware of such

precise information about the crash, and that the only explanation was that she had, indeed, communicated with the spirit world. The whole incident was widely taken as proof that such extraordinary powers do definitely exist. This was seen as a real vindication for the spiritualist community, who were often denigrated rather than supported by the establishment.

Garrett differed from many of her fellow mediums in that there were never any overtly theatrical physical manifestations at her séances. Rather than perform table-rapping or materializations, for example, she merely provided the opportunity to speak with the deceased. It was perhaps this simplicity of her approach that caused the establishment to support, rather than condemn, her activities, with many scientists risking their reputations to do so.

Following this widespread acceptance of her abilities, in 1932-33 Garrett agreed to participate in extensive psychoanalytical experimentation at the New York Psychiatric Unit and Johns Hopkins University, USA. In so doing, she revealed her open-minded attitude towards the human need to understand and explain the workings of the paranormal, which she embodied and, indeed, she had a very personal desire to gain a greater understanding of her own abilities. She lectured widely, founded the Parapsychology Foundation in 1951, and contributed her thoughts and findings to several publications, including the *International Journal of Parapsychology*, in 1959.

By the time of her death in 1970, Eileen Garrett was held in high esteem, not just for her skill as a medium, but also for her personal qualities. If she were alive today, she would no doubt continue to be as mystified as the rest of the world as to the precise nature of her psychic powers which, in spite of extensive investigations, remain to this day within the realms of the unexplained.

HELEN DUNCAN

Helen Duncan was the last woman ever to be charged with the crime of witchcraft in the UK. She was found guilty of this crime and imprisoned, despite having produced startling evidence of her genuine psychic abilities during her career as a medium. The most convincing example of this occurred in 1944, during the troubled days of World War II.

It is reported that, during one of her séances, Duncan appeared to bring forth the spirit of a sailor who had died while serving in the Royal Navy. The serviceman, who bore the words HMS *Barham* on his hat, told the assembled people that the ship had been sunk while in combat with the enemy. The relevance of this was not realized until the participants of the séance realized that they had been informed of this man's death before the authorities were even aware of it. The sinking of the HMS *Barham* was not announced until several hours after the séance finished and, indeed, it was initially denied that the vessel had been sunk at all.

Later that year, Duncan came under the scrutiny of the law. Fellow spiritualists have since alleged that this was due to the authorities' concerns over the possible risk to military security posed by her extraordinary powers. At that time, the Allied commanders were planning the D-Day invasion of Europe, and security was raised to unprecedented levels. Suspicion about Duncan's activities led to the police arriving at one of her séances, interrupting proceedings and searching the scene. Although they found nothing, she was nevertheless brought to court, where a variety of fraud

Helen Duncan was the last person in the UK to be prosecuted under the Witchcraft Act.

charges were levelled against her.

In a move that caused some consternation among the public, and outrage among Duncan's community of fellow spiritualists, Duncan was prosecuted under the Witchcraft Act of 1735, and imprisoned. The fact that the authorities were willing to use such an outdated and draconian law suggests a sense of desperation on their part, or at least an ulterior motive. Interestingly, the sentence of nine months that Duncan was given placed her neatly out of the picture until after the D-Day invasion had taken place, and not long after this, in 1951, the Witchcraft Act was repealed and replaced with the more modern and specific Fraudulent Mediums Act.

Once freed from jail, Duncan immediately began working as a medium once more. Yet her involvement with the police was not over, as in 1956 they again suspected her of wrongdoing. This time, they raided her séance in Nottingham while she was in a deep trance. She seemed to react very badly from the shock of being interrupted while in this state, and a doctor had to be called to treat her. Within five weeks of the raid, she was dead.

To this day, there is a campaign to clear the name of Helen Duncan among the spiritualist community, who are enraged by the way she was treated and by the nature of her untimely death. In light of such a large body of evidence of her particular abilities, it seems very hard to refute that she was indeed genuine.

HMS Barham sunk in military action in 1944. Before news of its end had been released, Duncan had seemed to communicate with the spirit of one of those who had passed away on board and announced the loss of the ship to everyone present at the séance.

EUSAPIA PALLADINO

Prior to the surge of scientific interest that took place during the Cold War, perhaps no medium had undergone quite such rigorous scientific scrutiny as the Italian psychic, Eusapia Palladino. This renowned spiritualist was investigated by over fifty scientists for more than twenty years and the vast majority of the tests proved that she was, indeed, genuine.

Born in Naples in 1854, Eusapia had a troubled childhood. Her mother died shortly after she was born and, when she was 12, her father was murdered. It was in the year following this incident that her unusual powers began to manifest themselves. While the young Eusapia was attending her first séance, the furniture was said to move towards her and even levitate, an act of telekinesis that was to set the pattern for what was to follow.

The tale of how Palladino rose to psychic prominence is surprisingly convoluted and begins in 1872 in London, long before she had ever set foot there. Here, the English wife of an Italian scientist named Damiani was attending a séance, at which a communication was made with a particular spirit who stated that there was a medium of prodigious talent residing in Naples, and that she was the reincarnation of his daughter. On their return to Italy, the Damianis resolved to seek out this medium. Their enquiries eventually led them to Eusapia Palladino, who was already well known in her community for considerable psychic powers.

In spite of this portentous message, it was still a considerable time before Palladino's talents came to be witnessed by the world at large. Finally, in 1892, word of her unusual abilities reached the famous Italian criminologist Cesare Lombroso, who decided to carry out some investigations into her abilities. After a long series of thorough tests, the initially sceptical Lombroso and his colleagues announced that Palladino was, indeed, a true psychic. This endorsement from one of the foremost Italian scientists of the day caused many learned people from around the world to travel to Italy

A painting of the famous medium Eusapia Palladino.

to witness her demonstrations for themselves, and from this point on, Palladino's fame was assured.

Descriptions of her séances reveal that Palladino was able to perform a remarkable range of psychic activities. Entering a deep trance, she would move furniture around the room, bring forth, out of nowhere, disembodied hands that might touch members of the audience, or convey messages through writing or tapping sounds. Observers noted that the nature of these events seemed to reflect her state of mind at the time, with more violence being demonstrated if she seemed perturbed during the session.

Almost all scientific observations indicated that Palladino was an authentic psychic, so there was naturally a great uproar when she was inspected by the Society for Physical Research in Cambridge, and was declared to be cheating. The scientific community was dismayed, particularly in view of the fact that so many eminent men had given her their backing. However, a subsequent inspection revealed that Palladino was genuine after all.

It is to science that sceptics turn in order to expose sham spiritualists and, therefore, the fact that the scientific establishment of the day ruled so overwhelmingly in Palladino's favour must count strongly towards her credibility. We must also remember the spirit at the London séance who first alerted the world to her powers, as well as her extraordinary early displays of telekinesis. All the evidence points to the fact that Eusapia Palladino was a genuine psychic phenomenon whose mysterious powers are, even today, an endless source of intrigue.

A table levitates during one of Palladino's séances.

MADAME BLAVATSKY

Madame Helena Petrona Blavatsky was a figure as controversial as she is remarkable, and her writings, views and predictions arouse heated debate and astonishment even today. To many she is considered a powerful psychic, a cultural messenger and even a prophet. As with all controversial figures in history there are those who attempt to debunk her incredible achievements and abilities, but when faced with the evidence, it is particularly hard not to believe that she was genuinely psychic. During her lifetime a wealth of literature by her and about her was created, and she brought about a revolution in Victorian spiritual thinking that affects us all today.

Madame Blavatsky was born in 1831 to a family of aristocrats in Dnepropetrovsk, Ukraine, although she spent most of the rest of her life travelling. The staff and servants of her family home later recalled how unusual she was as a child and how they credited her with possessing powers spoken of in their ancient rustic superstitions. She was reported to be a strange and troubled child, prone to sleepwalking, fits and headaches, all of which are common symptoms amongst those who have experienced visions or otherworldly communications.

By the age of 18 Blavatsky was married to a man much her senior, but she quickly grew tired of him and embarked on a life of adventure and travel, leaving her family and country behind. There are numerous versions of Blavatsky's life story, especially concerning the less documented part of her early years. In this time she was alleged to have borne an illegitimate child and to have been the mistress of numerous men. However, despite this behaviour, which was utterly scandalous for the era she lived in, Blavatsky still achieved great fame and respect in society. She was undoubtedly afforded this leeway due to her status as a person who was profoundly different.

Blavatsky spent most of her 60-year life travelling over huge expanses of the globe, studiously absorbing the culture and spiritual thinking of various different sections of humanity. Among the countries she visited were lands as diverse as Canada, Mexico, the West Indies, the USA, Japan, Egypt, and India to name but a few.

Many of the skills she acquired while on this enlightening world tour, were to have a bearing on her later life. She worked at one point with a circus and, at another, as an assistant to a medium who performed

A young Helena Blavatsky with her mother.

séances. However, it was her work alongside Eastern spiritualists that she claimed was the most influential force in her life.

Blavatsky told of how she spent several years in India, studying as the student of great spiritual masters. She claimed that several 'mahatmas' took her into their trust, and that she became their apprentice. Her unique abilities were recognized by these great mystics and she was granted unprecedented access to ancient mystical secrets reserved only for the initiated. It was from these roots that she explained her extraordinary abilities of prophecy and communication with the spirit world.

These Eastern travels were a crucially important aspect of Madame Blavatsky's life for more reasons than this, however, and have left us a legacy of knowledge even today. She stated that it was here that she acquired the most important knowledge of her life. With this spiritual learning as her base, she introduced the first real taste of the wisdom and understanding of Eastern religions to the Western world, in particular ideas of karma, reincarnation and the hidden higher powers of the mind.

On her eventual return to the West after her spiritual apprenticeship, Blavatsky propounded the idea of reincarnation – a concept that was totally alien to Western Judeo-Christian spiritual thinking. She explained how she believed in the spiritual journey of the soul through many different bodies on the road towards perfection. She did not believe in humans reincarnating as animals, but rather that the human soul slowly evolves, improving itself until it can gain extraordinary superhuman powers.

She maintained that a small number of these highly evolved superhuman beings existed in India and elsewhere and that they were guiding the fate of the world. The mythical paradise of Shambala is said to be inhabited by these luminous superhuman beings who have attained greatness after many reincarnated lifetimes. Blavatsky stated that they were the sole possessors of the hidden 'ancient wisdom' that

Blavatsky with Hindu Theosophists. Blavatsky travelled extensively in her life and took great influence from Eastern religions and philosophy.

The seal of the Theosophical Society on a door in Budapest.

originated from highly advanced human civilizations of the past. She insisted that they had been guarding this knowledge and using it to benefit mankind.

The nature of what she described endorses certain aspects of Eastern philosophy. Indian Yogis attempt to reach a higher state of consciousness through dedicated training and the application of their minds through meditation. Many such monks and Yogis are capable of extraordinary superhuman feats as a result of the mystical power they have cultivated within themselves.

Blavatsky was later to crystallize her view of this Eastern spiritual thinking, and combine it with her own sense of mysticism, into a system called the 'Theosophical Movement', which she founded with a number of her followers in 1875. The teachings of this movement are still adhered to by a number of people around the world today. According to Blavatsky herself: 'The chief aim of the ... Theosophical society [was] to reconcile all world religions, sects and nations under a common system of ethics, based on eternal verities'.

Blavatsky's aim was unity. It seems that she was seized with a kind of moral fervour, recognizing the inherent wisdom of this ancient and peaceful school of thinking. She realized that for any change to come about in wider society she must publicize this wisdom as much as possible. There is no doubt that this mission benefited greatly from all the publicity she received from her psychic displays.

In some of her demonstrations she was said to have materialized objects such as a cup and saucer. On other occasions she produced written words that were said to originate from the spirit world. The nature of her displays would vary hugely, demonstrating her array of skills and powers. Blavatsky claimed to be able to communicate with her distant Eastern masters by a kind of spiritual telepathy. At one stage she explained how she had seen visions of a tall Hindu who actually materialized before her in Hyde Park, and then became her personal guru and teacher. Claims of this kind were typical of Blavatsky, who liked to create as much mystery around her person as possible to advance her cause.

Some of this has been dismissed by the sceptical as trickery and stage-play, especially as she may have learnt various 'magic' tricks from the performers she worked with. However there is plenty of other evidence of her abilities that is not quite so easy to dismiss. For instance, her writings contained new explanations of world history that differed massively from the accepted view, and predictions for the future that appear to have the essence of truth within them. Despite seeming outlandish at the time, many of her assertions have been proved true, giving her abilities great credibility.

Blavatsky explained to her Victorian audience that much of the 'ancient wisdom' professed by her Eastern teachers actually originated from the great lost civilizations of the past, such as Atlantis. She first mentioned the lost city of Atlantis in her 1877 book *Isis Unveiled*, which sold out on the day of its publication. In the decade following this, the mystery concerning Atlantis became the talk of the Victorian world, with other authors and thinkers such as Ignatius Donnelly approaching the subject with intense intellectual curiosity. Even today there are scientists and explorers searching for traces of this mysterious lost culture.

In 1888 Blavatsky went into even greater detail in her next book *The Secret Doctrine*. In this book she displays a thorough knowledge of the deep-sea floor, describing details which were far beyond the known science of her day. Notably she asserted that the recently discovered Mid-Atlantic ridge continued under Africa and into the Indian Ocean. This has since been proved true, as the ridge is the boundary of a tectonic plate. What makes this so remarkable is that the Victorians had no idea of plate tectonics, and no means of verifying what she said. Technological advances in more recent times have revealed the extent of Blavatsky's genius.

Although this information may seem unrelated to her other teachings on Theosophy, it is actually tied in completely with her general world view. All that Blavatsky had learned from her masters was from a store of lost knowledge she referred to as the 'great ancient secrets', which had originated from lost civilizations such as Atlantis or Lemuria, and had been guarded for millennia. Only the initiated were allowed access to this knowledge. Blavatsky claimed that the philosopher Plato himself was an initiate of this secret advanced brethren, which is how he knew about the existence of Atlantis.

Blavatsky's prophecies of events that will befall our own culture make chilling reading. She predicted that there will be: 'a world destruction as happened to Atlantis 11,000 years ago ... instead of Atlantis all of England and parts of [the] NW European coast will sink into the sea, in contrast, the sunken Azores region, the Isle of Poseidonis, will again be raised from the sea'.

Although predictions of doom abound in history, when they come from a character as peculiarly convincing as Madame Blavatsky they cannot be ignored. What is more, scientific revelations and discoveries in the fields of climatology and meteorology have revealed the possibility that she may be right. At present the global climate is warming more rapidly than at any

The emblem of the Theosophical Society, as presented on an Indian centenary stamp from 1975.

Madame Blavatsky in pensive mood.

An image from Annie Besant, an early Theosophist, representing the thought-forms in the music of Gounod.

Madame Blavatsky predicted that in the Azores land would rise from the sea.

point in history. If this causes the polar ice caps to melt completely, it could have catastrophic ramifications for the world. Global sea levels could rise by several metres and low-lying areas of land, such as England or Holland, would be inundated, fulfilling the prophecy.

Blavatsky's predictions for the Azores also have definite potential to be fulfilled. The Azores is a particularly active geological area, with plenty of volcanic and tectonic activity. Although we cannot say that Blavatsky is correct, and land will rise from the ocean, she managed to pick one of the places in the world that this is most likely to happen. It is unlikely that she could have deduced this scientifically at the time, so we must assume that she gained this information from some supernatural origin.

Once again there is a mystery based on the inexplicable possession of advanced knowledge. When civilizations, tribes, or even individuals possess knowledge that is in advance of the science of the day, serious questions are posed about its origins. It becomes even more intriguing if they claim that this knowledge originates from a time before civilization is even believed to have existed. How could this knowledge exist without the prior existence of an advanced civilization such as Atlantis?

There is much about Madame Blavatsky's life and achievements that it seems impossible to answer fully. Yet there is the unmistakable ring of truth in much of what she said. The peaceful pursuit of meditation and spiritual advancement in Tibet still amazes many in the West, just as it did the audiences of Madame Blavatsky in the 1800s. Scientific predictions for the future seem to concur with some of her more doom-laden prophecies, and many of her assertions were proved true after her death, leaving us to wonder how she came to know such details. Lack of a better explanation means we must accept that she possessed these 'ancient secrets', and that she was one of the most amazing and mysterious characters in recent history.

According to Renier, everyone possesses their own unique energy field and we leave behind psychic 'fingerprints'. She uses psychometry to detect radio waves coming from an object left by its owner.

NOREEN RENIER

Clutching a single shoe to her breast, Noreen Renier summons up a picture of the appalling tragedy that befell its owner. She spills details of the disturbing scenes that fill her head into a nearby tape recorder, hoping that her words will bring about a breakthrough in a deadlocked investigation.

Noreen is a psychic sleuth, one of very few psychics who are recognized by some members of the police force as an asset in a tricky inquiry. The technique she uses is called psychometry, which allows her to sense the radio waves emanating from an object after it has been put aside by its owner.

According to Noreen, psychometry is something we would all be capable of doing, if only we used the whole and not just part of our brains.

Noreen speaks as a former sceptic. She was so convinced that paranormal claims were fake that she wanted to ban a psychic convention from the Hyatt Hotel in Orlando where she was public relations director.

'We all possess unseen energy fields. When we touch an object, we leave behind an invisible fingerprint.'

However, her view changed when a friend persuaded her to be more openminded. She met with a psychic called Anne Gehman who was able to describe her daughters, her hidden surgical scar, and the new chair in her office. This was compelling evidence that the supernatural world really existed.

Eventually she lost her job, admitting with good humour that this was something she didn't predict. She began a fortune-telling business in hotel foyers, clad in gypsy garb. Corny though this sounds, it gave her ample opportunity to hone her talents. As she grew in confidence, she put herself forward for scientific tests to measure her psychic skills. Since 1980, as a fully-fledged psychic, she has been helping the police with their investigations, either at their request, or of the families involved.

'Slowly, this "psychic stuff" began to take root in my life. I didn't understand it, but I couldn't deny it, either. I was completely captivated by the amazing new world that had opened in my mind. I started neglecting my job. All I wanted to do was practice what other people claimed they could do in the books I was reading.'

Noreen Renier, *A Mind for Murder*

CRIME SCENE - DO NOT CROS

Noreen Renier uses remote viewing to place herself at a crime scene to discover the details of what happened before recounting them to a forensic artist.

In addition to psychometry, Noreen uses remote viewing. That means that she is able to see, hear and feel the world through the senses of another. She can place herself as an eyewitness at the scene of a murder or amid the panic of a fugitive. In investigations, it is vital to take down all the details whilst she attempts to describe the events she is experiencing. Ideally, a forensic artist is standing by as she talks to sketch the face of the killer or rapist, and a tape recorder is running to capture her psychic advice.

Afterwards, the memories of her 'flashbacks' are erased from her mind and she returns to normality, sometimes for weeks at a time. As Noreen describes: 'It would be too much to be psychic all the time. So I've found a wrecked plane a thousand miles away, but sometimes I can't find my car keys.' She finds the experience very draining and limits herself to two cases a week. By and large, her work is carried out in the comfort of her own home. Relaxation is key to her success.

The first case that Noreen was involved in occurred when a small town was being terrorized by a rapist, and the local women asked for help. After visiting the homes of two victims, Noreen saw a man in a green uniform with a scar on his knee who drove a mystery vehicle that, for some reason, continued to turn around constantly. Although her intervention did not directly secure an arrest, her information was proven correct when the culprit was finally caught some months later. He did work in uniform, he was scarred and he drove a cement lorry, all of which Noreen had described.

One of her most impressive and high-profile predictions was that of an assassination attempt on US President Ronald Reagan. Speaking in January 1981 at the FBI academy, she said that in spring the President would suffer piercing chest pains. It was not a heart attack, she was sure, but a gunshot wound from which he would recover. Amazingly, on 30 March that year John Hinkley attacked Reagan, who did make a good recovery.

Mayhem ensued after an assassination attempt on President Reagan as he was leaving the Washington Hilton in 1981. Could events like these have been predicted, and maybe even prevented?

Tributes to Renier

'You definitely opened many eyes to the potential investigative tool of the psychic. Obviously, many a doubting Thomas had to revise his ideas concerning this somewhat esoteric area,' said Daniel Grinnan Jr. from the *Bureau of Forensic Science* in the Commonwealth of Virginia.

'Noreen never could have known this stuff beforehand and she was so accurate it was chilling,' retired Lt. Commander R. Krolak told *The Times Union* on 11 February 1992.

'It was kind of scary when we did find [the body], and it was almost exactly as she described it. I wouldn't say I'm a total believer, but I don't throw out anything they say.' So said Lt. Robert Miller in the *Port St. Lucie Tribune* on 19 May 1991.

Since then Noreen has worked on hundreds of cases across America and internationally. Sceptics point out that much of the information revealed by psychics is vague, so that it can be applied to a host of outcomes. Futhermore, they claim that the practice of psychometry can seriously damage vital evidence. Although the police accept more psychic advice now than ever before, they are generally sceptical of information provided by psychics. Their reluctance is understandable, especially since in the wake of any high profile homicide, they are deluged with calls from people claiming to be psychic.

Noreen is well used to a measure of scepticism, especially since she herself used to be a sceptic. Even now, she maintains that her skills are not foolproof and admits she thinks that psychic detectives should only be used as a last resort. Her aim is for a success rate of about 80 per cent. Often she does not know herself if the information she gives the police will be of immediate interest to an inquiry or whether it might help solve a crime at some point in the future. Psychic detection is an elusive skill, but sometimes an invaluable one.

JEANE DIXON

Jeane Dixon was a psychic, clairvoyant and astrologer who, during the course of her life, made a large number of predictions, with varying degrees of accuracy. One prophecy about which she was entirely correct, however, was her foretelling in 1956 of the assassination of President Kennedy, several years before it actually happened. It was only after this event that the world really started to pay attention to her remarkable psychic abilities.

Dixon was born in 1918 and, long before her famous prediction, had been working in the realms of the paranormal, using her powers to prophesy world events. She would foretell the future by means of dreams, in which spirit helpers would impart information to her. This method of prophecy is not uncommon, having been shared by a number of psychics over the years, but it is not the most reliable means of predicting the future as there can be confusion over the interpretation of certain visions.

Dixon's prediction of the Kennedy assassination was, indeed, initially vague – in fact, she did not at first actually name Kennedy as the victim. However,

Jeane Dixon had powers of prophecy and foretold a number of major world events – however not every prediction she made was accurate.

in subsequent predictions, she added more details: she foretold that a Democrat (which Kennedy was) would win the election and that Kennedy would either be assassinated or would die in office. Moreover, she backed up these predictions with a timescale that also proved to be correct.

Although Dixon is best known for her pronouncement on the Kennedy assassination, this was not the only event that she accurately foresaw. She also predicted other notable historic happenings, such as the Soviet Sputnik launch in 1957 and the Apollo rocket disaster that killed several American astronauts in 1967. In addition, she foretold that in the spring of 1989 the world would witness a shipping accident – and the Exxon Valdez oil disaster did occur at this time.

Some of Dixon's other prophecies were not quite so accurate, however. She wrongly predicted, in line with early thinking, that the Soviets would land on the moon before the USA, but of course the reverse happened. She also mistakenly foresaw an apocalyptic 1980s, in which a devastating meteor strike would hit the earth.

Occasionally, Dixon made a prediction that came very close to being reality, such as her prophecy that a third world war would commence in 1958. Although such a conflict did not actually take place, this period of our history was overshadowed to a large degree by the imminent threat of nuclear war.

Dixon also told of a plague that looked likely to descend on the USA during the late 1970s – while this was of course inaccurate, some have suggested that she may have been catching a future glimpse of the arrival of AIDS in the Western world and its devastating effects on public health.

Many have wondered whether it is possible to credit Jeane Dixon with psychic abilities when the verity of her predictions has varied so much over time. Her advocates would argue that the future does not actually run along a set course, but is flexible, and that there are numerous possible realities. Dixon, they maintain, simply presents us with one of these potential scenarios. If this is the case, then it would certainly go some way towards explaining how she was so very nearly correct in her predictions of a third world war.

It is certain that debate will always surround figures such as Dixon, because of the inexplicable nature of their amazing powers. Believers will see patterns of truth in the psychic's predictions, while sceptics will continually point out their inaccuracies or ambiguities – it has to be said, however, that even the famous Nostradamus was proved wrong on some accounts, but he is still classed as one of the world's genuine clairvoyants.

As long as mankind exists, there will be a desire to know the future before it actually happens, and it seems that certain special people, with extraordinary gifts, will be able to divine these truths, defying the very laws of time in order to do so.

President John F. Kennedy in the limousine in Dallas Texas, moments before he was shot in 1963. Dixon predicted the tragic assassination in 1956.

NINEL KULAGINA

During the Cold War, each side conducted extensive secret research into any area that might give them an advantage over the other. With no subject deemed too unusual to be exploited, both the CIA and the KGB investigated the possibility of using paranormal powers, such as telepathy, for intelligence-gathering purposes. Anyone demonstrating special psychic abilities was seized upon and exploited in the quest for victory.

Ninel Kulagina, was one such character. She was a housewife from St Petersburg who was studied by the Soviets for more than ten years because of her paranormal abilities.

During this time she revealed her amazing powers of telekinesis – the ability to move objects by the power of the mind alone. The fact that Kulagina was investigated for such a long period of time seems to indicate that she was nothing other than entirely genuine.

Film footage still exists of Kulagina causing a compass needle to move by focusing energy through her fingertips. Another of her displays of telekinetic ability was to move matches across a table, or to cause a pile of them to collapse purely by the power of a concentrated stare.

But it is the later displays of her remarkable talent that reveal why the authorities were so interested in her powers. In one experiment, an egg was cracked into a saline solution, and she proceeded to separate the yolk from the white by her powers of kinesis.

In another demonstration which was particularly sinister, Kulagina is said to have stopped the heart of a frog from beating, purely by the power of her mind. To the Cold War scientists, this must have been an incredibly exciting breakthrough in human mental ability and this aptitude would have presented all sorts of horrific possibilities to men who were determined to emerge victorious from this most sinister of global conflicts.

Performing these incredible feats took a serious physical toll on Kulagina, and it is this that apparently persuaded the Soviet doctors of the authenticity of her feats.

After she had demonstrated her telekinetic prowess, she reported having experienced a sense of hot energy running up and down her spine and emanating from her hands. During this time, her pulse would apparently race to over 200 beats per minute – the equivalent of doing strenuous exercise, and she is even reputed to have lost weight through such a display. The activities would also affect her blood pressure and she spoke of feeling dizzy and exhausted for several days afterwards, experiencing headaches and blurred vision. Eventually, she was forced to end her involvement with the research after suffering a heart attack, no doubt brought on by her exertions.

Sceptics have argued that all the evidence that exists about Kulagina could have been nothing more than a huge conspiracy on the part of the Soviet powers to alarm the western world, especially as, during the Cold War years, each side went to a great deal of effort to deceive the other over the extent of the scientific progress being made. Perhaps this is just one more example of such an attempt.

It is impossible to know for sure what secret scientific discoveries were actually made during the era of the Cold War, but there is certainly some very convincing evidence to suggest that Ninel Kulagina was possessed of very remarkable, and mysterious, powers.

Ninel Kulagina was believed to have the the power of telekinesis, the ability to move objects using only her mind.

DANIEL DUNGLAS HOME

Daniel Dunglas Home was a leading medium of the 19th century.

Daniel Dunglas Home is considered by many spiritualists to be one of the most gifted mediums of all time. During his unusual career, he demonstrated his psychic prowess on countless occasions and is remarkable for the incredible range of his ability. Whereas most spiritualists tend to specialize in the demonstration of a particular type of paranormal activity, nothing seemed beyond the reach of Home's amazing powers.

Home was born in 1833 in Edinburgh, Scotland and, in common with many spiritually gifted people, his talents first manifested themselves during his childhood. His aunt described how, even as an infant, his cradle could be seen to rock itself, unassisted. As a child, he experienced some significant psychic events, and at one stage is said to have seen a vision of his mother that coincided with her death in another city.

Such remarkable powers could not protect him from illness, however, and he was a very sickly child. At the age of nine, he moved from Scotland to Connecticut, USA, to live with his aunt, and it was here that he was diagnosed with tuberculosis.

One of the results of this condition was that Home's childhood was a particularly solitary one, during which time he came to believe that he was surrounded by the spirits of the dead. In fact, he would maintain throughout his life that he was supported by certain spiritual benefactors, and that it was these beings that were responsible for his paranormal displays.

The young Home's fascination with the supernatural and the strange happenings of his early years worried his God-fearing aunt, who believed that he must be possessed by the devil. Sadly, while he was still in his mid-teens, he was cast out of her house, and from this time on was forced to seek his fortune in the only way he knew how – by working as a professional medium. He would often be offered board and lodging by a patron in exchange for the performance of séances and rituals, at which he would demonstrate his impressive abilities.

Home's repertoire was huge – apart from

Dunglas Home levitates in front of an audience. He frequently displayed powers of telekinesis and communing with the spirits at the séances he hosted.

communicating with the deceased, he would also conjure up from nowhere whole arrays of spectral lights and music. Another of his skills was his extraordinary ability to shrink himself in size, or elongate his body, a phenomenon that was witnessed, and verified, by several people at once.

It was perhaps his displays of telekinesis, though, that were the most remarkable. At several séances, Home caused tables and chairs to move of their own accord and on one occasion he was able to levitate a table to such a height that he could walk beneath it. He maintained, however, that these demonstrations could not actually be classed as telekinesis, for the actions stemmed not from the power of his own mind, but from the actions of friendly spirits with whom he was able to converse easily.

Home made it publicly known at this time that he believed the vast majority of mediums to be fraudulent, and so he took measures to prove that, unlike them, he was genuine. In contrast to other practitioners of the time, Home would conduct his séances in well-lit rooms, or even out of doors. When he demonstrated his ability to move items of furniture, he would challenge the audience to take hold of his hands and feet to prove that he was not touching anything. Many found his displays utterly convincing, particularly those in which he would summon up spirit hands that would then either touch members of the séance, or write out personal messages for them.

Despite such public demonstrations of his talents, it was not until 1852 that Home's career, quite literally, took off. In a display that seemed to set him apart from his fellow spiritualists, Home showed how he was able to levitate off the ground for a prolonged period of time. According to the account of a journalist, F. L. Burr, who witnessed the event, Home levitated no fewer than three times, and on the last attempt actually rose up to touch the ceiling. Home later asserted that the levitation should be attributed to the power of his spirit companions, who had chosen to lift him into the air in this way.

Home even performed a séance for Emperor Napoleon III of France, where he claimed to contact the spirit of Napoleon Bonaparte.

Home's fame spread far and wide, and he set off on a European tour, eventually reaching Russia, where he married. During his travels, he performed séances for some of the leading figures of the day, notably Emperor Napoleon III of France and the Empress Eugenie. Both were amazed by his abilities. At one stage, Home even appeared to make contact with the deceased Napoleon Bonaparte, who signed his name on paper. The Emperor was enormously impressed by this, announcing to all that the handwriting was genuinely that of Bonaparte himself.

Arguably the most famous and impressive of Home's feats was performed in London, at the home of Lord Adare, in 1866. Apparently without warning, Home slipped into a trance and began to levitate. He then proceeded to float out of one of the open windows before drifting back in through another. This demonstration ensured Home's popularity and fame, especially as the assembled audience was possessed of considerable credibility and influence.

What is clear is that Home was a supremely talented individual. Some sceptics have asked, however, whether his skills as a medium were genuine or whether his abilities lay more in the area of deception. It has been suggested that Home may have induced some powerful kind of mass hallucination in his audiences through the power of suggestion.

Nevertheless, when one takes into account the

The prominent scientist Sir William Crookes investigated Home's powers for two years, but failed to find evidence of fraud.

consistency of his displays, the huge numbers of people convinced of his authenticity and the lack of any evidence to the contrary, it seems highly unlikely that Home was anything other than a true psychic.

Home was so confident of his own abilities that he agreed to subject himself to some rigorous investigations. Sir William Crookes, a well-known scientist of the day with a particular interest in spirituality, studied Home's activities over a two-year period. During this time, Home apparently managed to make an accordion play while it was sealed inside a cage which had been specially designed by Crookes to block out the magnetic energies that he believed were the root of Home's power.

Finally, Crookes was forced to admit that he could find no scientific explanation for Home's remarkable powers.

At this point, his recurrent tuberculosis forced Home to retire. His powers had not only been displayed and witnessed, but they had been inspected scientifically and there is still no explanation that is more plausible than his own. He was indeed a uniquely gifted individual, and an astonishing manifestation of the latent powers of human consciousness.

JOSE ARIGO

During his lifetime Jose Arigo became renowned for his inexplicable psychic talents, which he used to great effect in healing the sick and injured. Indeed, many of his actions were even proclaimed as miracles by his admirers. Sadly, however, his attempts to use his amazing healing powers for the good of mankind were eventually cut short by his imprisonment, when the authorities ruled that his activities were contrary to the law.

Born in 1918 into the peasant class of Brazil, Arigo could never have anticipated the level of international fame he would eventually enjoy as a result of his unusual gifts.

He first became aware of his abilities while visiting a dying relative; the whole family had assembled to bid their farewells to the woman who was suffering from a life-threatening tumour. However, as the priest read out the last rites, Arigo recounted how he felt strangely compelled to take action. Seizing a knife from the kitchen, he cut into the woman and removed the tumour on the spot. Amazingly, she made a rapid recovery, and it was after this that Arigo's community realized that they were fortunate enough to have a remarkable psychic healer in their midst.

Such was the poverty in Arigo's neighbourhood that there was very limited access to doctors and medicine. It was not surprising, therefore, that the news of his healing ability spread rapidly, and soon he was being asked to treat large numbers of people. Although initially reluctant to put others at risk by operating on them, Arigo quickly discovered that he was able to repeat the success of his first operation on numerous occasions.

Jose Arigo seemed to possess a remarkable ability for healing.

Although such healers have been known to exist in other communities, particularly in the Philippines, rarely has this talent been used with such success, or without recourse to hidden methods. Many of these healers have claimed that they are able to heal the sick because they are somehow blessed, often seeing themselves as conduits for the Holy Spirit. In contrast, Arigo's explanation for his healing powers was an unusual one, as he attributed his skills to the fact that when he was operating he would become possessed by the spirit of a deceased German physician, Dr Adolphus Fritz.

It is difficult to find an alternative explanation for Arigo's remarkable abilities, since he was very poorly educated and certainly had no medical knowledge whatsoever. The only other possibility is that Arigo invented the story of Dr Fritz in order to deflect attention away from the incredible powers that were actually entirely his own. Whatever the truth, Arigo continued to credit the success of his work to the spirit of Dr Fritz throughout his entire life.

Arigo had practised his healing on a large number of people before he came to the attention of the authorities. The medical establishment had serious concerns about the unsanitary nature of his operations and his complete lack of any medical qualifications.

Eventually, in 1936, he was arrested for the illegal practice of medicine, after which he was fined and sentenced to eight months in jail. The establishment was not prepared, however, for the huge level of public support for Arigo – the extent of which eventually caused the President of Brazil to step in and offer him an official pardon.

Almost 30 years later, however, in 1964, Arigo was not so lucky, and he was forced to face his sentence. Although the prosecuting judge, Filippe Immesi, was amazed by a demonstration of Arigo's powers, he was forced to conclude that Arigo was nevertheless breaking the law and sentenced him accordingly. While in jail, Arigo still continued his healing practices, believing at this stage of his life that it was his mission to help as many people as possible.

Some time later, Judge Immesi visited Arigo in jail, where the ensuing episode impressed him so much that he subsequently wrote an account of what he witnessed. He described how he had seen Arigo perform a cataract operation on a woman's eye with a pair of nail scissors. Despite the fact that the operation was conducted while the patient was fully conscious, she displayed no signs of pain. No type of disinfectant or antiseptic was used, Arigo merely wiped the scissors on his shirt before cutting into the woman's eye. After he had performed the operation, Arigo said a short prayer before pronouncing that the woman was cured.

Arigo died following a car accident in 1971. In the course of his lifetime, he had healed many thousands of people who, without his intervention, would surely have died.

Modern science is unable to offer an explanation as to how Arigo was able to practise with such an astonishing degree of success, often using in his surgery whatever unlikely implements came to hand at the time.

One suggestion is that he might have been using the placebo effect on his patients in the same way as that practised by African witch doctors. These remarkable people trick patients into thinking they have been healed and, because the patients' belief is so strong, they go on to make a full recovery.

However, this method could not explain the incredible level of success that Arigo managed to sustain over so many decades. Belief in his power of healing will take many years to fade.

Sculptures of the Twelve Prophets, carved by Aleijadinho, in the Brazilian town of Congonhas. Brazil had its fair share of individuals with inexplicable powers, including Jose Arigo.

THE GIRL WITH

'New Light Sees Through Flesh to Bones' was the headline in one newspaper when, in 1896, Wilhelm Conrad Roentgen (1845-1923) unveiled his new x-ray machine. His discovery was to change the course of modern medicine. But in 1997, some 100 years later, a young Russian girl claimed to see inside human bodies without the benefit of technology, using her eyes alone.

As a young girl growing up in Saransk, the capital of Mordovia some 480km (298 miles) east of Moscow, there was little to mark Natasha Demkina out from her playmates. But all that changed when, aged ten, she confessed to her mother that she could 'see' beneath her skin, inside her body. Under Natasha's penetrating gaze, her mum's bones, sinews and blood-pumping veins were all startlingly apparent.

Natasha began to use her unexpected talents to diagnose ailments among friends and family. Her startling success rate soon led people to call her 'the girl with x-ray eyes'. As her reputation spread, Natasha was confronted with more 'patients' than ever. She returned from school each day to discover a line of people outside her house, hoping that she would identify health problems undetected by doctors. She began to charge people a small fee. Natasha dreamed of going to medical school, and when her family realized how expensive this would be, the cost went up again.

Saransk, Russia – Natasha Deminka's home town.

X-RAY EYES

Some Natasha enthusiasts claimed she had offered her diagnostic opinion to 10,000 people.

Her bizarre visual surgery finally attracted the interest of an international television company, who asked her to appear on air and expose her skills to camera scrutiny. Ringing in the ears of the television producer were the words of her proud mother Tatyana, 'She has never been wrong in six years.'

In May 2004, the show arranged for Natasha to be put to the test. Unfortunately for Natasha, the notoriously sceptical Committee for the Scientific Investigation of Claims of the Paranormal was involved in drawing up the conditions of the test.

Seven people were selected as subjects for the experiment. Six had different but specific medical issues that would show up on an x-ray, for example, one had an artificial hip while another had internal metal staples. The seventh was, medically speaking, intact. Natasha was given cards with illustrations of the conditions she was expected to identify. Descriptions of them were written in both Russian and English. All seven were expected to remain seated during the test, although Natasha generally saw patients while they were on their feet. The authors of the test decided Natasha would be deemed successful if she got five out of seven diagnoses correct. The result of the test would not provide definitive evidence that Natasha possessed supernatural powers, the authors decided, but would only determine whether her 'gift' warranted further study. The experiment was to take place in New York, a long way from home for 17-year-old Natasha.

The test was expected to be over in just over an hour, but in the event it lasted four hours. This was unusual, since up until then Natasha had completed most consultations within ten minutes. Furthermore, she was thought to have chatted to friends and family

'At first I was disgusted. Then I became used to it. It seems normal now and, if I don't see anyone for a while, I miss the experience.'

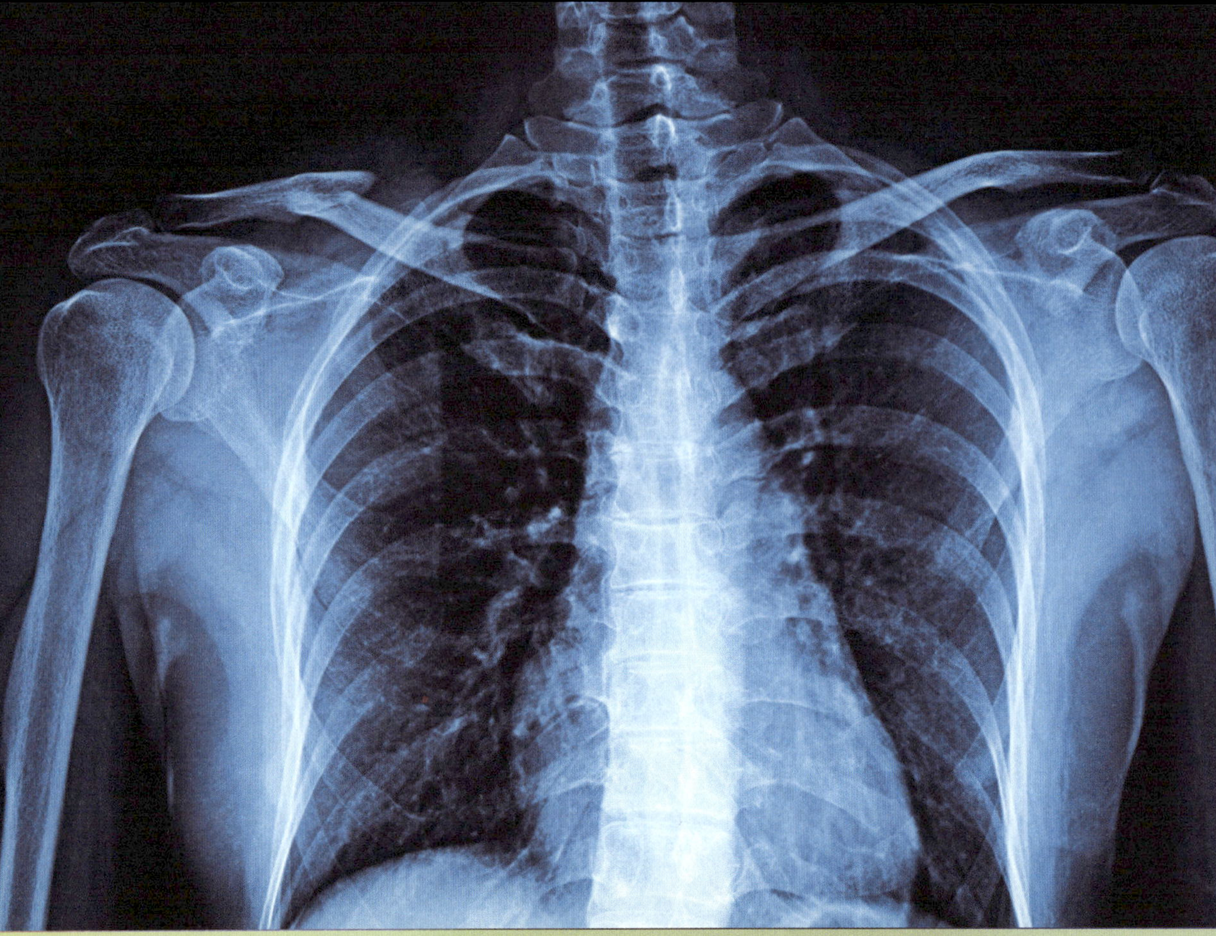

An x-ray image showing the spine, ribcage, shoulder and arm bones of a patient. Could Natasha really see into people as clearly as this?

on her mobile phone, when the rules stated she was to talk to no one.

At the end of the test Natasha was found to have made four correct diagnoses rather than the necessary five. It proved, said Andrew Skolnick, one of the authors of the test, that her gift as a 'medical intuitive' should be called into question. Natasha had contravened the rules of the test, he said, and taken hours to produce a result that simply was not very impressive. Among the medical conditions she had missed was a man with a metal plate in his skull that was reportedly visible to the naked eye.

Assertions that she could make cellular diagnoses were disputed by those who organized the test, who said a drawing she submitted of a particular rogue cell was in fact nothing like the real thing. The test organizers suspected Natasha of making 'cold readings', a technique honed by fortune tellers of old. It entails the psychic or healer bombarding their subject with questions and alighting on minute clues to draw sweeping conclusions about the state of their health.

In the face of such questioning, subjects tend to focus on the correct statements while disregarding the flurry of false information offered beforehand, especially if they are eager to believe. Furthermore, they said she was operating from a position of strength, since it was almost impossible to prove her wrong. In many instances it would take an autopsy to determine whether her medical diagnoses were correct or not.

As far as the test organizers were concerned, all these factors meant that Natasha was no longer of interest.

But Natasha's supporters took issue with the results of the test. Her figures, although not up to the required

No ordinary eyes: after undergoing international scrutiny of her abilities, Natasha attended university in Moscow to study medicine.

standards of the panel, were nevertheless statistically significant. There was only a one in fifty chance of achieving such a result, which surely put it beyond mere chance. 'Why is it that if I get five out of seven I pass but if I get four I'm a total failure?' asked a dejected Natasha. Furthermore, Natasha was operating under stressful, unsupportive conditions when all psychics work better in a relaxed atmosphere. Her sympathizers felt that she had been ambushed by sophisticated sceptics with a vested interest in branding her claims as false. Their reputations were, at the end of the day, rooted in disproving paranormal events rather than endorsing them. This was the same crowd who had decided Uri Geller, a famous spoon-bending psychic with armies of devotees, did not have sufficient skill to warrant further investigation either. In the meantime, Natasha's talents had come under scrutiny elsewhere. She was judged to be entirely convincing by a variety of different audiences, not least *The Sun* newspaper in Britain. Nor is she the only person in the world today to apparently possess x-ray vision. There are a number of psychic healers who make similar claims and offer a list of success stories to back their case.

Afterwards Natasha sank from the limelight, concentrating on her studies at medical school. She was following the ambition she had as a child, to become a doctor, before she attracted so much international notoriety. As she put it, 'The dream is, if I preserve my gift, to use it but on the basis of proper medical knowledge.' With medical training behind her, Natasha may yet return to confound her critics.

CHAPTER 4

SEERS AND ORACLES

The desire to predict the future is deeply rooted in human nature. People have always been fascinated by the art of prophecy and throughout the ages have attempted to discern what the future might hold for them. Sometimes they try to achieve this by consulting an individual who possesses the unique ability to see into the future – a seer or an oracle.

There are many different methods of divination, which are practised by societies all over the world. Belief in the power of the prophet is strong, as case after case demonstrates that there is some truth behind this mysterious phenomenon.

THE DELPHIC ORACLE

The Pythia entered a trance before delivering her prophecies in highly cryptic language, which would be interpreted by the high priests of the temple.

Throughout history, the role of the oracle has figured prominently, as it has in numerous tales of classical mythology. Of all the famous oracles, perhaps the best known and respected was that found at Delphi in Greece.

The oracle at Delphi was at the shrine of Apollo, the Greek god of fine arts and prophecy. Set high on the hillside of Mount Parnassus, it occupied a prominent position, reflecting the esteem in which it was held in Greek culture.

According to legend, Apollo took control of Parnassus when he was child, by killing Python, a huge dragon snake, in the battle between the gods of the sky and the earth. Apollo then assumed the form of a dolphin (*delphis* in Greek, from which the shrine derived its name) and journeyed out into the ocean to capture some sailors who were appointed his first high priests.

Apollo delivered his prophecies at Delphi through various prophetesses, or sybils. The sybil, who was always a mature woman who had lived a pure life, would take on the name Pythia upon being appointed, after the python slain by the young Apollo.

When the prophecies were made, Pythia would enter a trance before delivering her predictions in riddles. These were then translated and interpreted by the high priests and then they would be relayed to the waiting supplicants.

Upon arriving at Delphi, these supplicants would have registered and paid a fee to make an appointment. They would then have been required to purify themselves in the Castalian spring, where a bathing trough still exists, and travel up the Sacred Way to the shrine. A sacrificial offering in the form of a sheep or goat would have been made and the entrails examined for omens by priests. When the pilgrims finally reached the sybil, they were allowed in, one at a time, to ask for her predictions.

The Delphic oracle was visited over a period of almost 2,000 years, during which time countless prophecies were delivered on subjects ranging from wars and matters of state to personal affairs, births and deaths. The supplicants came from almost every level of society, a factor that demonstrates the regard in which prophecy was held in the everyday life of those times. The power and influence of the oracle can also be seen in the art and literature of the period. Not only does it figure in Virgil's *Aeneid* and Homer's *Odyssey*, but in Sophocles' story of Oedipus, the oracle predicts to the King and Queen of Thebes that their son Oedipus would kill his father and marry his mother. As the dramatic events unfold, the prophecy is fulfilled, evoking questions about fate and morality that are relevant to this day.

The ruins of the Temple of Apollo at Delphi, where the oracle made her predictions.

NOSTRADAMUS

In the 16th century Nostradamus gained a measure of notoriety for making uncannily accurate prophecies. But even he could not foresee that his words would have such a long-lasting effect, remaining pivotal in the beliefs of many people up to five centuries after his death.

The words penned by Nostradamus during his many years as a seer have been translated, pored over and debated. Still, no one is sure how much weight to lend them. While some of his predictions appear wildly speculative and never came to pass, others seem to have neatly summed up events with spine-chilling clarity. Nostradamus was born Michel de Nostredame in St Rémy de Provence on 14 December 1503. He was from a prosperous middle-class family and his father is generally described either as a lawyer or grain merchant. Young Michel proved to be a brilliant young scholar, showing particular skill for languages and the sciences. He also read voraciously. The family had recently converted from Judaism to the more prevalent Roman Catholic faith, so Michel grew up with a thorough knowledge of both belief systems.

However, Nostradamus' first passion was medicine, and at the age of 18 he entered the University of Montpelier to train as a physician. He was able to put his new-found expertise to good use, since the bubonic plague, or the 'Black Death' was ravaging medieval Europe, and doctors were in great demand At the time his approach to patients was radical. Donning the protection of a rudimentary mask, he treated people using good hygiene and herbal poultices rather than the barbaric practice of 'bleeding' patients that brought them to the brink of death.

Nostradamus married and fathered two children, but his medical skills were not sufficient to save his young family from the clutches of the Black Death. After the death of his wife and children, the bereft Nostradamus became a wandering scholar, travelling throughout southern France and Italy.

It was while he was in Italy that the

Nostradamus (1503–1566) couched his prophecies in a mysterious combination of French, Latin, Greek and Italian, in order to avoid condemnation by the Catholic Inquisition.

N° 9. — 10 mai 1909. — Publication bi-mensuelle paraissant le 10 et le 25. — Prix : 20 Centimes.

LA VIE MYSTERIEUSE

Directeur : Professeur DONATO

ASTROLOGIE — MAGIE — CARTOMANCIE — CHIROMANCIE — GRAPHOLOGIE — SPIRITISME — MAGNETISME

RÉDACTION ET ADMINISTRATION : 12, rue N.-D. de Recouvrance, Paris-2e. — MAGASIN DE VENTE : 4, rue St-Joseph, Paris-2e.

NOSTRADAMUS REÇOIT CATHERINE DE MÉDICIS

Voir, page 130, LE TAROT DE LA REYNE, par Mme DE MAGUELONE.

Nostradamus alarms Catherine de Medici, Henri II's queen, with his predictions.

first sign of his future career became apparent. He came across a group of Franciscan monks herding cattle and had a strong premonition of the future, which led him to kneel down and address one of the monks as 'your holiness'. Years later the monk, Felice Peretti, became Pope Sixtus V (1520-1590).

When Nostradamus reached the age of 44, he ended his itinerant lifestyle and settled in the Provencal town of Salon. He married a wealthy widow and began his career in prophecy in earnest. His aim was nothing less than to prophesy the future of mankind, and eight years later he produced the first of more than a dozen books of predictions. The books are called *Centuries* because each is made up of a hundred verses, or quatrains.

Nostradamus was a devout man, but he saw no conflict between his religion and his prophecies. However, he knew that others would not share this openminded attitude. This was the age of the Inquisition, and anyone suspected of anti-Catholic sentiment was mercilessly punished. The art of peering ahead in time would certainly not sit well with the cruel monks who led the Inquisition. So he set about disguising his predictions by couching them in a mysterious combination of French, Latin, Greek and Italian. Furthermore, he used metaphors and anagrams to produce baffling and impenetrable riddles. He did this, so he told his son, so that the enlightened folk of the future could decipher his messages. But as yet, the generation he was pinning his hopes on has not emerged.

Despite the mysterious nature of the predictions, Nostradamus' *Centuries* became popular reading material, particularly amongst nobility and royalty, and his reputation grew ever greater. During his lifetime, he came to prominence for one prediction in particular, which gained him both friends and enemies.

The Young Lion will overcome the older one on the field of combat in a single battle,
Inside a cage of gold his eyes will be put out,
Two wounds made one,
He dies a cruel death.

(Century 1, Quatrain 35)

Just four years after this prophecy, King Henry II died during a joust when a lance pierced his gilded visor and caused two mortal injuries. Many believed that Nostradamus had caused the death of the King, and demanded that the prophet be tried for heresy. Fortunately for Nostradamus, the king's widow, Catherine de Medici, did not share their view. She was so impressed by his powers that she hired him as physician to her son and heir.

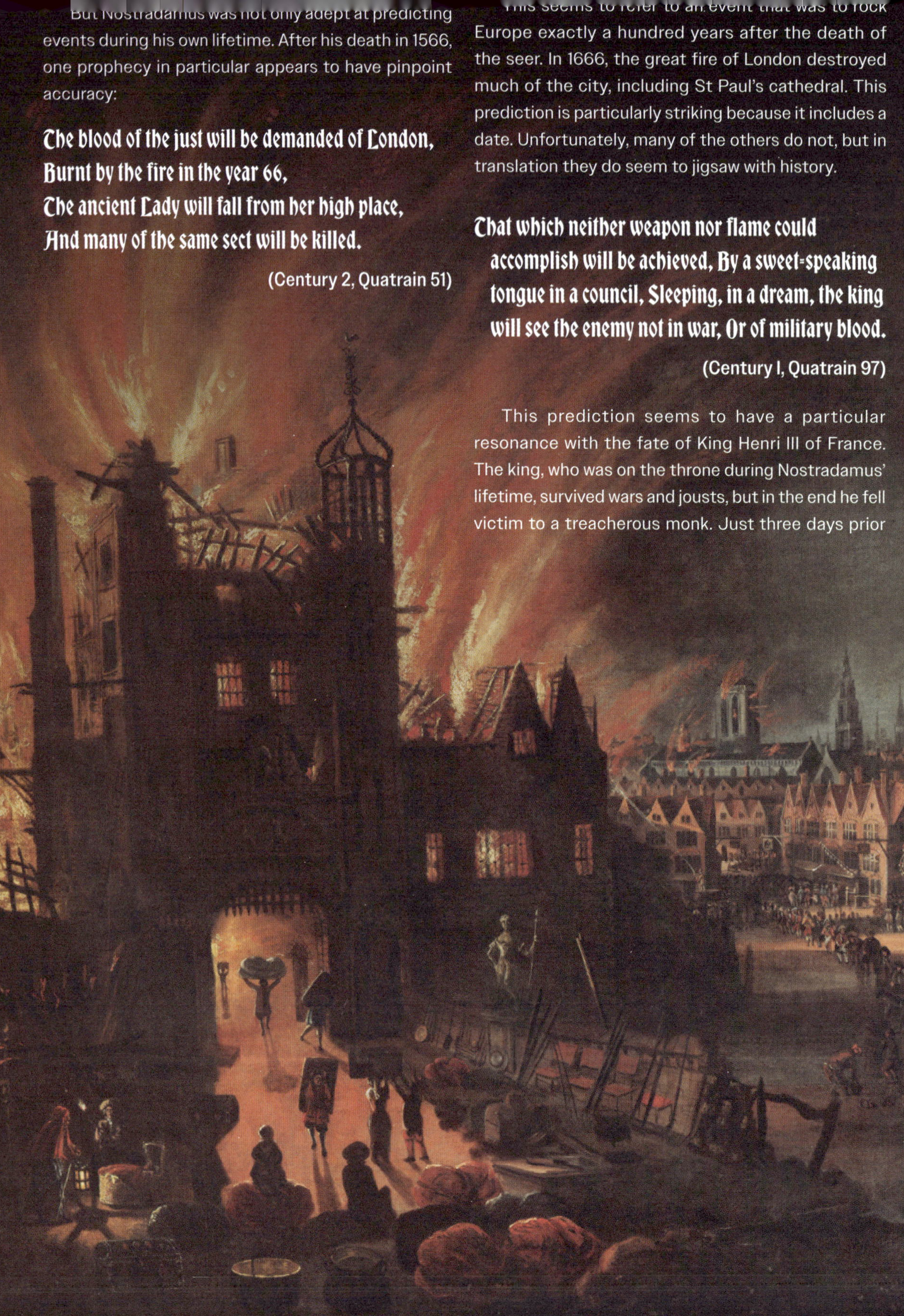

But Nostradamus was not only adept at predicting events during his own lifetime. After his death in 1566, one prophecy in particular appears to have pinpoint accuracy:

The blood of the just will be demanded of London,
Burnt by the fire in the year 66,
The ancient Lady will fall from her high place,
And many of the same sect will be killed.

(Century 2, Quatrain 51)

This seems to refer to an event that was to rock Europe exactly a hundred years after the death of the seer. In 1666, the great fire of London destroyed much of the city, including St Paul's cathedral. This prediction is particularly striking because it includes a date. Unfortunately, many of the others do not, but in translation they do seem to jigsaw with history.

That which neither weapon nor flame could accomplish will be achieved, By a sweet-speaking tongue in a council, Sleeping, in a dream, the king will see the enemy not in war, Or of military blood.

(Century I, Quatrain 97)

This prediction seems to have a particular resonance with the fate of King Henri III of France. The king, who was on the throne during Nostradamus' lifetime, survived wars and jousts, but in the end he fell victim to a treacherous monk. Just three days prior to his death, he had a premonition about what would happen in a dream.

The rejected one shall at last reach the throne,
Her enemies found to have been traitors,
More than ever shall her period be triumphant,
At seventy she shall go assuredly to death, in the third year of the century.

(Century VI, Quatrain 74)

Surely this refers to Queen Elizabeth I of England, who was the least favoured of her father's children. But when she finally ascended the throne in 1558, in the face of Catholic opposition, her reign was indisputably glorious. She did indeed die aged 70, and the year was 1603.

Although many of Nostradamus' predictions tally with historical events to a startling degree, others are tantalizingly vague and they are not in chronological order. Sceptics have drawn attention to the prophet's ambiguous language, and the fact that he is thought to have copied other prophecies current in his era. The subject matter he chooses is invariably war or natural disasters, and these will always be a feature of history. The critics claim that if the cryptic messages of Nostradamus can be applied to real events, then it is nothing more than co-incidence. Take, for example, the quatrain thought by many to refer to the coming of Hitler:

Beasts wild with hunger will cross the rivers,
The greater part of the battlefield will be against Hister,
He will drag the leader in a cage of iron,
When the child of Germany observes no law.

(Century II, Quatrain 24)

Incredibly, this quatrain does at first seem to sum up the events of World War II during Hitler's dictatorship and to allude to the savage Nazi troops swamping Europe and humiliating conquered leaders. However, Hister is also the exact name of an area close to the Danube. So the prediction can be read with two meanings, although with historical hindsight, it makes better sense when Hister is read as Hitler.

Some of Nostradamus' prophecies have been wrong, most spectacularly the one that implied a catastrophic war would break out in July 1999. Yet despite the ambiguity that surrounds his predictions, thousands of people give due respect to Nostradamus, believing his case has been proven at least in part. With long grey hair and a beard, he certainly must have looked the part of an accomplished seer. Whilst other prophets of a similar kind have been forgotten, the reputation of Nostradamus has flourished through the centuries since his death. And since his predictions continue until 3797, he still has plenty of time to be proved right.

One premonition that he got exactly right was his own death. 'You will not see me alive at sunrise,' he told his assistant on the evening of 1 July 1566. True to his word, by the following morning he was dead.

One of Nostradamus's quatrains appears to refer to the rise of Adolf Hitler – however he writes the name as 'Hister', leaving room for doubt.

THE SANGOMA

Deep in the heart of southern Africa there lives a tradition of healing and divination that is integral to African culture, and is as respected today as it was thousands of years ago. The extraordinary powers of Sangomas, or diviner priests, are a revered alternative to more modern medicine, and their predictions are remarkable in their accuracy. It is estimated that around 200,000 such diviners are practising today, helping more than 84 per cent of the southern African population.

The role of the Sangoma varies and can be divided into two primary categories, although these are by no means rigid. The principal kind of Sangoma is the ancestrally designated diviner who communes with the ancestors, usually by entering a trance, to predict the future. The second type of Sangoma is the herbalist or doctor, who uses traditional methods to cure the sick and has not been called by the ancestors. However, these boundaries are often blurred, as the ancestrally designated diviner is often also a herbalist, consulting the ancestors for guidance on treatments and cures.

Novices (thwasas) begin their training by enduring and surviving an 'initiation illness' (ukuthwasa). This signals that the ancestors, or deceased spirits, have called them to their vocation. The relationship between the novice and the ancestors is forged during the recovery from the illness, and the person assumes a new identity and role in life.

The ancestral link is crucial to the cures and readings that will be made by the Sangoma, as it is believed that the ancestors are the messengers from the higher

A Sangoma performs a spiritual reading by interpreting the thrown bones.

power, or 'Supreme Being', acting as a link between deity and man. The Sangoma, in turn, provides a mouthpiece for the oracles, and carries out their instructions, in much the same way as the sybils of Roman times delivered prophecies from Apollo.

The deliverance of these oracles fulfils a major social and political function, as the prophecies provide an acceptable arena for debate about issues that may otherwise be taboo or politically dangerous. Predictions are made on subjects ranging from the state of the crops and the weather to personal problems and health issues. Sangomas maintain that illness can be attributed to one of three main causes – the ancestors, witchcraft and 'pollution' (for example, menstruation or miscarriage). Once the root of the problem has been established, the process of healing can begin.

The trance state entered by the diviner is usually central to the process of delivering the oracle. This condition is achieved through a wide variety of ritualistic methods, including rhythmic drumming, clapping and dancing, the inhalation of herbal medicines (muti) such as snuff, and the burning of incense (indumba). The attire of the Sangoma is also very important, and he will often wear elaborate ostrich feather head-dresses, and tie rattles and beads to his body.

Upon entering the trance, the Sangoma often starts to shake, and his breathing becomes more erratic as the ancestors enter his body. The rhythmic rituals result in hyperstimulation of the body, while the irregular breathing brings on hyperventilation, both of which are said to 'open' the body and mind to allow access to the ancestors. The men then use 'bones' (shells, coins, dice and twigs) as part of the divination ritual, which are thrown on to an impala skin. The position and alignment of the scattered objects are then interpreted, providing the Sangoma with the information required to deliver the oracle or to cure the patient.

The predictions provided by these revered men have become such a normal part of everyday life in these regions that their magical elements tend to be overlooked.

In western culture, however, the repeated fulfilment of the Sangomas' prophetic pronouncements and incredible cures continues to baffle and astound.

A Sangoma in Zambia performs a blessing during a ceremony.

THE BRAHAN

Deep in the mists of the folklore of the Scottish Highlands lies the character of Coinneach Odhar, the 'Brahan Seer'. This enigmatic figure's uncannily accurate powers of prophecy and his eventual trial for witchcraft made him renowned across the land and continue to amaze people to this day.

With little in the way of written evidence about the seer, his actual identity is unclear. Indeed, many of the tales about him have been preserved through oral tradition alone. The only official documents uncovered to date that might relate to this figure are two Commissions of Justice ordering the prosecution for witchcraft of a Keanoch Owir in 1577. However, this date is almost a century earlier than the period described in more traditional tales of the seer's prophesying, and seems unlikely to relate to the same man.

Local legend identifies the seer as Kenneth Mackenzie, a labourer born in Baile-na-Gille on the Isle of Lewis around 1650. It is said that he lived at Loch Ussie in Ross-shire, where he worked on the Brahan estate, the seat of the Seaforth chieftains, from about 1675. As the last, and most famous, of his fulfilled predictions specifically relates to this family, it seems likely that Mackenzie was the true Brahan Seer (*aka* Coinneach Odhar).

Many of the prophecies made by this figure related to the geographical region in which he lived, where the fulfilment of his predictions can be seen to this day. As many as 150 years prior to the construction of the Caledonian Canal, Coinneach Odhar is reported to have told a listener: 'Strange as it may seem to you this day, the time will come, and it is not far off, when full-rigged ships will be seen sailing eastward and westward by the back of Tomnahurich, near Inverness.' As, at the time of the premonition, the area in question consisted of rolling hills, the listener deemed what he had heard to be so preposterous that from that point on he ceased all contact with the seer.

Another visible example of the seer's prophecies lies in the parish of Petty, where a huge stone once marked the boundary between the estates of Culloden

The Brahan Seer memorial stone at Chanonry Point, Fortrose, Scotland.

SEER

and Moray. In 1799 this colossally heavy stone inexplicably moved some distance into the sea. How or why this occurred remains a mystery, but whatever the cause, the event was specifically foretold by the seer, who predicted: 'The day will come when the stone of Petty, large though it is, and high and dry upon the land as it appears to people this day, will be suddenly found as far advanced into the sea as it now lies away from it inland, and no one will see it removed or be able to account for its sudden and marvellous transportation'.

The seer seems also to have been adept at

The Seer prophesized the bloody Battle of Culloden.

predicting numerous important events in the history of Scotland, such as his premonitions of the carnage wreaked at the famous battle of Culloden. While walking in the vicinity, he is said to have stated: 'The bleak moore shall, ere many generations have passed away, be stained with the best blood of the Highlands'.

He also accurately foresaw the demise of the clan Mackenzie of Fairburn and its 16th-century Fairburn Tower, which stands high on the ridge between the Orrin and Bonon river valleys. At the time at which the prophecy was made, the Mackenzie clan, presided over by a rich and powerful chieftain, was enjoying success and stability. Nevertheless, the seer made the now-famous claim: 'The day will come when the Mackenzies of Fairburn shall lose their entire possessions; their castle will become uninhabited and a cow shall give birth in the uppermost chamber'.

Unthinkable as this may have seemed at the time, this prophecy has since been fulfilled to the letter. A few generations after the prediction was made, the family lost its power and wealth, and the tower was eventually abandoned, fell into disrepair and was taken over by a farmer, who used the upper floor for storing hay. One day, according to numerous eyewitness reports from 1851, a pregnant cow followed a trail of dropped hay up the precarious staircase to the upper level. Having become stuck, the cow gave birth to her calf right there on the top floor, just as the seer had predicted.

This was not the only fall from greatness accurately predicted by Coinneach Odhar, since he foretold the end of the male line of the Seaforth clan as a result of the premature deaths of all four sons. He also stated that all of the last lord's possessions would be 'inherited by a white-coiffed lassie from the east and she is to kill her sister'.

The Brahan Seer stone in Craig Wood is inscribed with the following: 'The shadow over Culloden will rise and the sun will shine brighter.'

And so it happened that, upon the death of the last Lord Seaforth, the estate was passed to the eldest remaining daughter, Mary, who was married to Admiral Hood and lived in the East Indies for many years. Upon the admiral's death, Lady Hood returned to her family home wearing a white coif, a traditional Indian mourning garment. Some years later, she lost control of the pony carriage in which she and her sister were travelling, and her sister died.

Coinneach Odhar did not live to see the fulfilment of this prediction, however. Over the years, suspicion about the seer had grown, with his mysterious powers being linked with witchcraft and the dark arts. His fate was sealed when he told Countess Isabella Seaforth, wife of the third Earl of Seaforth, that her husband was having an affair with a Frenchwoman. This news apparently so enraged Isabella that she ordered that he be tried for witchcraft. At the end of his trial the Countess had claimed that, in view of his powers of witchcraft, the seer's soul would not be fit for heaven. Upon hearing his sentence, the Brahan Seer had responded with one final prediction. He declared that upon his death, a dove and a raven would meet in the air above his ashes and would instantly alight on them. If, he said, the raven alighted first, then the Countess would be correct. However, if the dove should alight first, then his soul would go to heaven, while hers would go to hell. He was found guilty and executed by being pitched into a barrel of burning tar. According to legend, the spectators were astonished when the two birds did appear above his ashes, and awestruck when the dove alighted first.

Many more of the Brahan Seer's predictions have since been proved accurate. Whatever his real identity, it would seem that he really did possess truly mysterious powers of prophecy.

The seer worked for Kenneth Mackenzie, the third Earl of Seaforth. He sealed his fate when he informed the Earl's wife that her husband was having an affair.

EDGAR CAYCE THE SLEEPING PROPHET

Edgar Cayce is one of the most famous seers of recent times. During the course of his remarkable life, he gave in excess of 14,000 readings on more than 10,000 different topics, ranging from personal health and emotional issues to the lives of ancient civilizations and natural disasters. He is the subject of many hundreds of scientific works, and is read by curious minds the world over, in an attempt to unravel the mystery of his incredible powers.

Born in 1877 in rural Hopkinsville, USA, Cayce exhibited early signs of his unusual gifts when he baffled his teachers by absorbing vast amounts of information simply by 'sleeping' on his schoolbooks. Upon leaving school, he became a photographer, but tragedy was to strike him at the age of 21 when he was informed that he was suffering from a rare condition that would cause the gradual paralysis of his throat, and

Edgar Cayce, psychic healer and 'sleeping prophet'.

subsequent loss of speech. His miraculous recovery from this devastating illness was to be the first of Cayce's incredible cures. Having entered the same hypnotic sleep as that used to absorb information from his schoolbooks, Cayce was able to divine the cure to his illness. To the astonishment and bafflement of his doctors, his suggestions for treatments were totally successful and he made a full recovery.

Having discovered this amazing gift, Cayce quickly realized that he could use it to help others, and he soon became famous throughout the USA as a great healer. The healing process would begin with his establishing the name of the patient, after which he would enter his hypnotic sleep. He would then search to re-establish contact with the patient, before conducting a long conversation with him or her, prompted by questions from his attendant wife, to divine the symptoms of the illness. His secretary would note down everything he said in order that his response to the medical problem could be recorded.

Having established himself in this way, Cayce began to explore other areas of his hypnotically induced powers. In 1923, while working in a photographic studio in Selma, Alabama, Cayce met a printer, Arthur Lammers, who was to alter the course of his prophesying. Lammers was deeply interested in the subject of metaphysical philosophy, a topic far beyond the possible scope of Cayce's knowledge. Having heard about Cayce's remarkable powers, Lammers was keen to see what answers he might divulge to fundamental metaphysical questions. In this way, he hoped, great areas of uncertainty for mankind, such as the mystery behind the meaning of life, might be clarified.

Cayce agreed to go ahead with this experiment, and produced more than 2,500 'Life' readings over the rest of his life. These 'Life' readings related to information about a person's past life, and were distinct from his 'Physical' readings, which pertained to medical diagnoses and cures. However, these readings induced in Cayce a personal dilemma and crisis of faith. Raised as a devout Protestant, he had difficulty in accepting intuitive information relating to subjects such as reincarnation, which ran contrary to the Christian message.

After a while, though, Cayce managed to reconcile himself with these differences and continued with his work. He subsequently declared that the basis for all the great religions was surprisingly similar, as all the people of the world were united by a collective unconscious.

The 'Akashic record' was a supposedly infinite source of wisdom and information that Cayce claimed to be able to access.

Cayce claimed that the Sphinx dated back to 10,500BC, nearly 8,000 years earlier than the date usually accepted by archaeologists.

Cayce maintained that it was by tapping into this unconscious, or 'universal memory of nature', that he was able to make such a large number of predictions and readings. However, he was sceptical over suggestions that he was able to gain access to an infinite source of collective wisdom, known as the 'Akashic record'. This was, and still is, a contentious idea, and there was no scientific method by which it could be proved, other than by the fulfilment of his prophecies.

Cayce had a remarkable level of insight into past civilizations such as those of ancient Egypt and Atlantis, and this was a subject of great personal interest to him. One of his claims was that the Sphinx had been built in 10,500BC and that a 'Hall of Records', concealed beneath Atlantis, would be discovered in the late 1990s. Although the latter prediction has not yet come to fruition, many of his other insights are proving to be more accurate.

Cayce's intuitive insights into the nature of our climate seem to be becoming ever more true. Just as he predicted, there has been a marked increase in recent years in the intensity and frequency of natural disasters as storms, earthquakes and droughts. For example, a great storm has occurred every decade since the 1960s, when, previously, violent weather of this kind used to take place approximately only once every 500 years.

Another of his climatic predictions related to the imminence of polar shift, a switch in the magnetic polarity of the earth that will have catastrophic

Edgar Cayce's readings during his trances were carefully recorded and remain available in the Edgar Cayce Association for Research and Enlightenment (A.R.E.) Library in Virginia Beach.

consequences for the planet. Scientists today believe that Cayce's prognostications may prove to be correct, and that just such a devastating switch could occur.

Similarly, Cayce's prediction of the destruction and submergence of certain parts of the USA is also proving a very real concern among both meteorologists and scientists. Recent information has revealed that one flank of the Cumbre Vieja volcano on the island of La Palma, in the Canaries, is unstable and could plunge into the ocean during the next eruption of the volcano.

This would mean that almost 20km^3 of rock, weighing 500 billion tonnes, could fall into the water to a depth of more than 6km (3.7 miles). The effect of this would be the creation of an undersea wave more than 600m (1,969ft) high, which within five minutes would rise to the surface to form a huge tsunami, more than 1.5km (4,921ft) high. This would then disperse in all directions to form a 100m (328ft) wave travelling at the speed of a jet aircraft, which may have the capacity to devastate the east coast of the United States, the Caribbean and Brazil. The events of 26 December 2004 make this prediction even more alarming.

With global warming already evident, and modern technology confirming Cayce's predictions of polar shift and global devastation, it seems that this relatively modern seer was in possession of some truly remarkable gifts. How or why he obtained these incredible intuitive powers, however, remains a mystery that may never be solved.

The sinking of RMS *Titanic* is such a dramatic story that it is still being told today, all over the world. Most people are aware of the main causes of the tragedy – the freak iceberg and the shortage of lifeboats – but very few realize that, 14 years prior to the accident, a book was published that set out almost the exact details of the entire incident.

The Wreck of the Titan, or *Futility*, written by a little known author, Morgan Robertson, appeared in print in 1898. Receiving little attention, the book tells the story of a 70,000-tonne 'unsinkable' ocean liner named the SS *Titan*, which hit an iceberg on its fourth voyage across the Atlantic. The ship, bearing a number of wealthy and powerful dignitaries, was equipped with fewer than half the necessary lifeboats, and consequently more than two thirds of the 2,500 passengers on board perished in icy waters when the liner sank.

The parallels with the true story of the RMS *Titanic* are immediately apparent. Moreover, there are further, uncanny, similarities between the fictitious and real vessels, in details such as the weight of the ship, the nationality of the principal shareholders involved, the time of the impact and the number of lifeboats on board.

Incredibly, this was not the only time that a prediction was made about the fate of the *Titanic*. A few years prior to the publication of *The Wreck of the Titan*, a similar story had appeared in a newspaper article. A prophetic note by the editor at the end of the piece warned that 'this is exactly what might take place, and what will take place, if liners are sent to sea short of boats'.

In a chilling irony, this editor was one of the very passengers who perished when the RMS *Titanic* sank beneath the waves 20 years later.

Could this really be merely a cruel twist of fate, or was some higher power at work?

The Titanic departing on its maiden voyage.

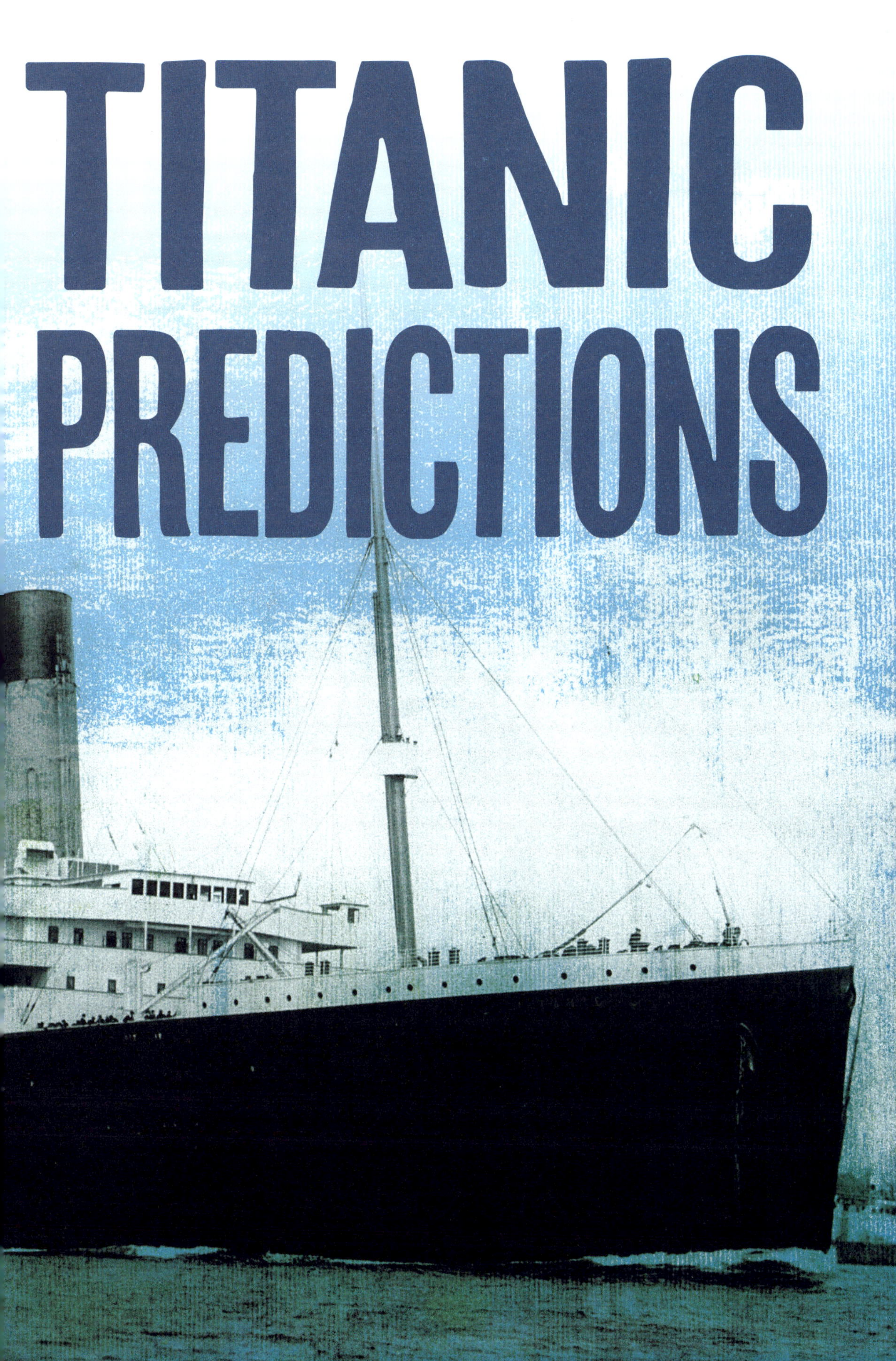
TITANIC
PREDICTIONS

THE UNKNOWN

Early in World War I came the discovery of a man who was remarkable for his powers of prophecy, making a series of astoundingly accurate predictions about events that would occur during, and after, both World Wars. Very little is known about this individual, other than that he was French, and he appeared to be a holy man. Whoever he was, his unique gifts have baffled experts for many decades.

In 1914, two German soldiers captured a lone Frenchman in the Alsace region of France. They imprisoned and questioned him, and it was during this interrogation that the extraordinary predictions were made. One of the soldiers, Andreas Rill, was so amazed by what he had heard that he wrote detailed accounts of the incident in letters to his family.

The unknown prophet predicted not only that the war was going to last for five years, but also that Germany would lose. There would then be a revolution, followed by a period of great prosperity in which, amazingly, money would be flung out of windows to lie untouched on the ground.

He said that, during this period, an antichrist would be born, who would begin a nine-year reign of tyranny in 1932, passing new legislation and secretly impoverishing the people of Germany. Preparations for a second war, that would last three years, would commence in 1939, and this time Italy would be allied to Germany, rather than fighting against it as it had in the previous conflict. Despite this, however, Germany would again lose. The German people would then rise up against the tyrant and his followers, and 'the man and his sign would disappear'. In a year containing the numerals '4' and '5', Germany would be surrounded by its enemies and destroyed.

Germany would be torn apart and a new man would emerge to lead and raise the new Germany...Every day there are new laws, and many will suffer or even die as a result. The time begins around 32 and lasts nine years ... everything goes by one man's dictate – he says – then comes the time 38, are invaded ... and worked to war. The war itself ends badly for the man and his followers...

The 1936 Nuremberg Rally. The captured Frenchman claimed that a reign of tyranny would begin in Germany in 1932.

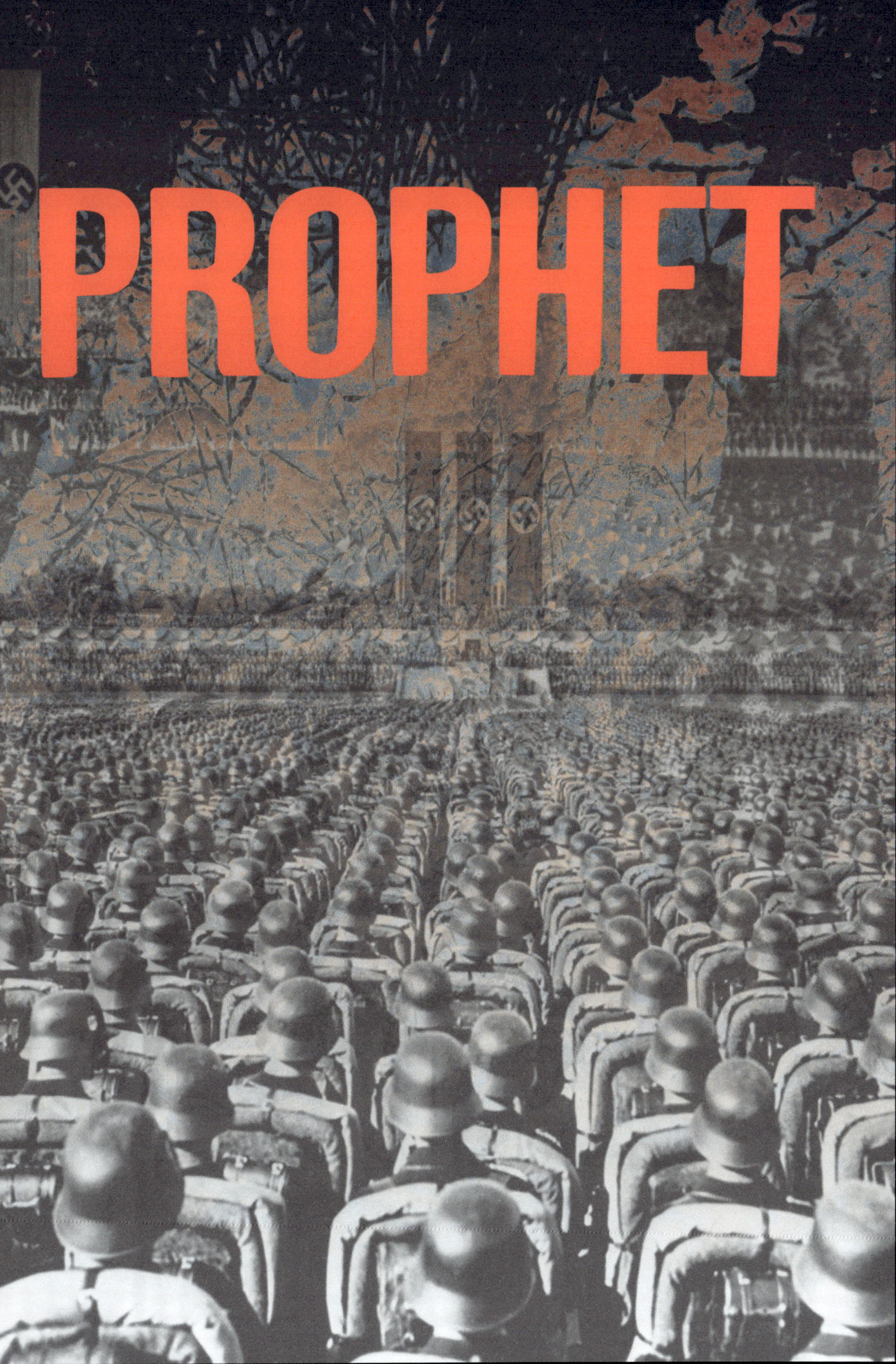
PROPHET

History proved the amazing veracity of these predictions. World War I, in which Italy fought against Germany, did last five years, and Germany did lose. This was by followed by inflation in which the German currency became so devalued as to be worthless.

Adolf Hitler's rise to power began during the 1920s, and in 1933 the National Socialist German Worker's (Nazi) Party commenced its oppressive reign, with Hitler at the helm, despite the fact that they had only 37 per cent of the vote. The Nazis then passed the Enabling Act, allowing Hitler to pass any new law he so desired, thus effectively signalling the demise of democracy and the dawn of dictatorship.

Preparations for the start of what was to be World War II began, as predicted, in 1939 when Germany invaded Poland. This conflict lasted until 1945, when the Germans were surrounded and forced to surrender. Hitler committed suicide and the arrival of the Allies resulted in the end of the reign of the Nazi party.

Rill was amazed to watch history unfold in line with the prophet's statements and, as time went by, the letters to his family became famous for their contents. Indeed, at one point they almost resulted in Rill's internment in a concentration camp due to their predictions about the imminent rise of a dictator.

The letters then lay dormant during the turbulent years of World War II, surfacing only briefly in 1950 when they appeared in a mission journal, published by a Father Frumentius Renner. This publication passed almost unnoticed and no attempts were made to check the authenticity of the letters or establish the identity of the unknown prophet.

The letters then arrived at the Freiburg Institute for Border Areas of Psychology and Mental Hygiene. Here, the accuracy of their contents provoked such suspicion that forgery was suspected and, accordingly, the documents were subjected to extensive testing and scrutiny by a team of expert criminologists. Following these investigations, it was declared that the letters were the genuine documents that Rill had sent home to his family back in 1914.

It was then decided to try to locate the mysterious seer, not an easy task as Rill had died. Professors Hans Bender and Elber Gruber traced Rill's movements in

The unknown prophet accurately predicted that World War II would end in 1945 with the defeat of Germany.

The parapsychologist Hans Bender carefully investigated Rill's movements in hopes of identifying the mysterious prophet.

an effort to establish the locality in which the man had been arrested. They conducted interviews with Rill's family, learning from his son that the visionary had apparently been a rich man who had given his wealth away in order to join a holy order. His son also remembered that his father had himself attempted to locate the nameless prophet in 1918, while posted in the town of Colmar. Upon arriving at the nearby monastery in Sogolsheim, he was reportedly told that the man had died.

The results of these interviews and their own painstaking detective work led the two professors to believe that this monastery had indeed been the last residence of the prophet.

After consulting monastery records, they established that he may have been Frater Laicus Tertiarius, who had died in 1917, not long before Rill's visit. This man seems to have stayed at the monastery as a guest rather than as a monk, which supports the theory that he had indeed been a rich man and consequently would have been barred from joining the brotherhood.

While it is true that this prophet did make some predictions that were not eventually realized, this may have been the fault of inaccurate recollection of the details by Rill, or even to linguistic errors on the part of the Frenchman while speaking German.

Overall, the accuracy of his predictions is truly astonishing, especially in view of the fact that the prophet could have had no knowledge about events that would only take place decades after his death.

How this anonymous seer achieved his prophetic visions is a mystery, and can only be attributed to the incredible powers of foresight.

THE HITLER HOROSCOPES

Countless history books have recorded, analysed and discussed the events that occurred before, during and after World War II, but, of these, few mention the significant part that astrology and prophecy played in determining the course of history. It is now known that both Stalin and Hitler frequently consulted seers and mind readers, even though, officially, they had forbidden the employment of such mysterious powers. In Nazi Germany, in particular, occultists suffered harassment and persecution, in common with all other minority groups.

Prior to the outbreak of war, a prophet and astrologer, Karl Ernest Krafft, was gaining great respect in Germany among his contemporaries. Born in Basle in 1900, Krafft was highly numerate, especially in the field of statistics, and was also passionate about astrology. However, it was the publication of his book, *Traits of Astro-Biology*, that was to raise him to such an extent in the estimation of fellow prophets and occultists. In this work, Krafft expounded his theory on predicting the future, which he termed 'typoscomy'. Essentially, this maintained that a person's destiny could be predicted on the basis of his or her personality.

When the war commenced, Krafft's privileged position was placed in peril. However, his life changed dramatically when a remarkably accurate prediction about Hitler brought him face to face with leading members of the Führer's command. Krafft foresaw that Hitler's life would be in peril at some point between 7 and 10 November 1939. In fact, he was so sure of this that on 2 November of that year he wrote to Dr Heinrich Fesel, a close acquaintance of Himmler, warning him of Hitler's impending fate. Fesel, not wanting to be associated with the prophet, filed the letter away without mentioning it to Himmler.

On 8 November a bomb exploded in the Munich beer hall just 27 minutes after Hitler had left the building. When the story became known, Fesel immediately supposed that Krafft must have been involved in the plot to kill the Führer, and so gave the letter to Hitler's right-hand man, Rudolf Hess.

Krafft was immediately arrested by the Gestapo, but they found him innocent of conspiring to kill Hitler. At this point, word of Krafft's remarkable powers reached the ears of Josef Goebbels, head of the Ministry for Propaganda, who had recently become fascinated with the works of Nostradamus. Goebbels ordered that Krafft be employed to decipher Nostradamus' complex quatrains and extract any references which could be inferred as good omens for the Third Reich and which could be used for propaganda purposes.

Then, in 1940, Krafft was called to give a horoscope

reading for Hitler. In this, he advised that a planned attack on the USSR be postponed until a later date. In spite of the fact that he had not actually met Krafft personally, Hitler followed his recommendation and waited until the following June before launching Operation Barbarossa.

The success of the attack on the USSR in the early days of the offensive seemed to prove Krafft's prediction to be correct, although this ultimately proved unsustained.

Krafft then insisted that it was imperative that Germany secured victory by 1943 at the latest, or else the war would be lost. Although history was to reveal the accuracy of this prophecy, the result for Krafft was that he was imprisoned. Hitler was enraged by his prediction, and cited it as the reason for the sudden defection of Hess in 1941. As a result, all occultists and astrologers were rounded up and put in prison.

Upon his release in 1942, Krafft was ordered to study the horoscopes of Allied leaders in order to provide his leaders with vital information about the enemy. Among his many readings was his divination that Montgomery would prove a stronger enemy than Rommel, an insight which proved to be correct.

His final, accurate, premonition – that a bomb would destroy the propaganda ministry in Berlin – resulted in Krafft being tried for treason. After languishing in prison for several years, he eventually contracted typhus and died in 1945.

The remarkable accuracy with which Krafft made his predictions seems undoubted proof of his oracular powers. In fact, Krafft's abilities so impressed the Allies that they attempted to find a seer of comparable skill to assist them in much the same way as Krafft had helped the Nazis. The fact that they were unable to do so demonstrates how rare and precious Krafft's talent really was.

Karl Ernst Krafft gave horoscope readings to Hitler. He came to the Führer's attention after accurately predicting an attempt on Hitler's life in November 1939.

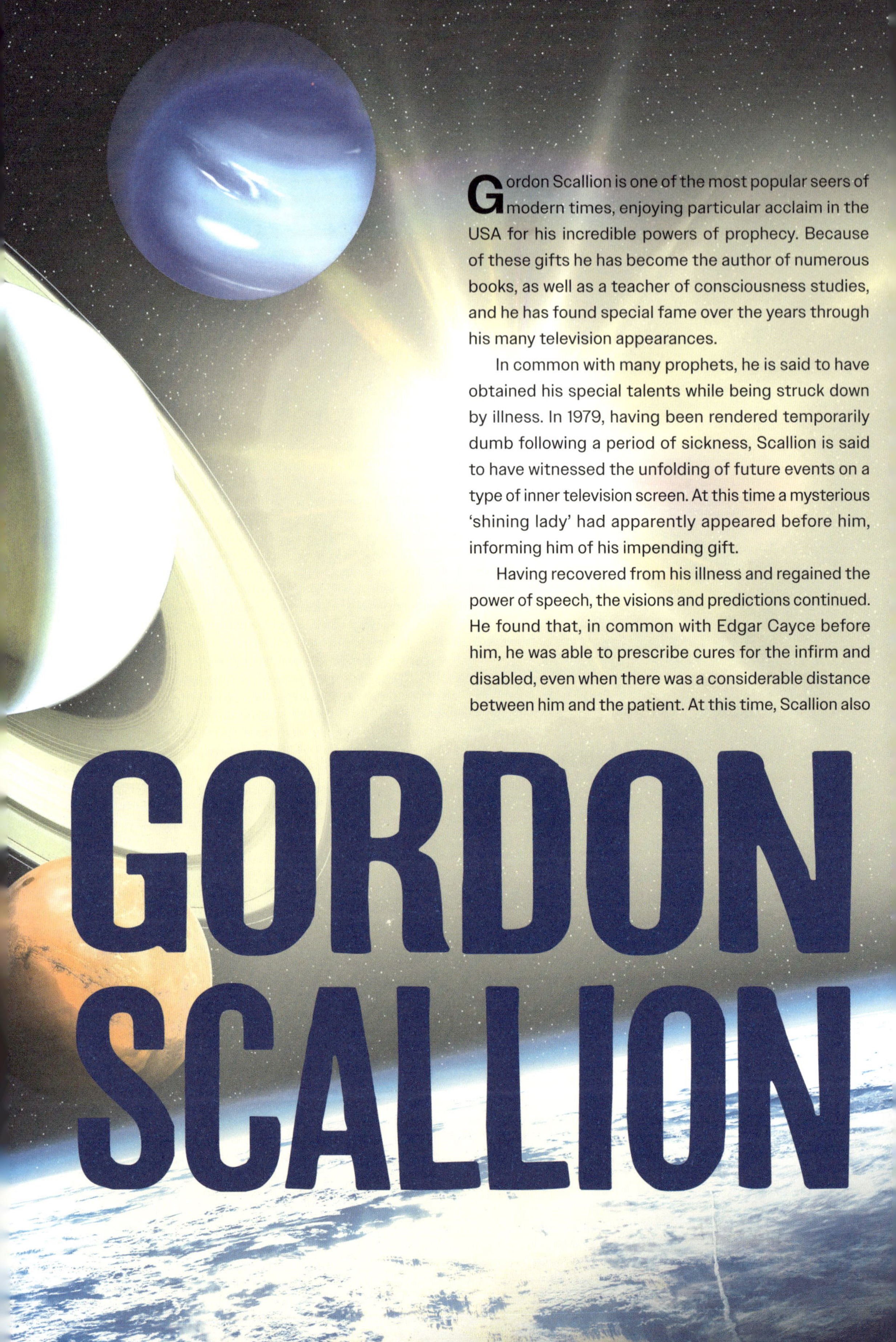

GORDON SCALLION

Gordon Scallion is one of the most popular seers of modern times, enjoying particular acclaim in the USA for his incredible powers of prophecy. Because of these gifts he has become the author of numerous books, as well as a teacher of consciousness studies, and he has found special fame over the years through his many television appearances.

In common with many prophets, he is said to have obtained his special talents while being struck down by illness. In 1979, having been rendered temporarily dumb following a period of sickness, Scallion is said to have witnessed the unfolding of future events on a type of inner television screen. At this time a mysterious 'shining lady' had apparently appeared before him, informing him of his impending gift.

Having recovered from his illness and regained the power of speech, the visions and predictions continued. He found that, in common with Edgar Cayce before him, he was able to prescribe cures for the infirm and disabled, even when there was a considerable distance between him and the patient. At this time, Scallion also worked as a lecturer, and founded the Matrix Institute, where records of his visions are stored to this day.

After some years spent working as a healer, Scallion noticed that his talent seemed to be shifting, and he found himself able to predict the changing state of the earth.

One powerful vision involved the physical body of the earth, which appeared to him to be in some distress. It seemed that a bulge had formed in the earth's core, which was altering its mass. Ultimately, Scallion maintained, this would result in a massive upheaval at the earth's crust, causing dramatic changes to the position and size of the continents.

Scallion reported these predictions in his newsletter, 'The Earth Changes', and the continental shifts are also illustrated on a new map of the world. He warned that these disruptions at the earth's crust will lead to huge earthquakes, with the eventual submergence under the sea of large tracts of land. He also envisioned polar shift and the emergence of new landmasses.

Of all his numerous predictions, however, perhaps none was more impressive than his foreseeing of Hurricane Andrew in August 1992. The details of his prophecy were remarkably accurate, especially over matters such as the range of dates on which the hurricane might strike, the wind velocity, the path of the storm and the extent of the damage caused.

In his newsletter, he also accurately predicted the 1985 Mexico City earthquake, the 1988 election of President Bush, the 1987 stock market crash and a series of major earthquakes and volcanic disturbances both in California and Japan.

Further endorsement of his accuracy seems to have been given more recently by the scientific press, which has revealed its concerns about the possibility of impending polar shift and the potential occurrence of a mega tsunami. On 26 December 2004 the world witnessed the powerfully destructive forces that Scallion predicted. This event, combined with the increasing occurrence of violent weather and devastating earthquakes, would seem to be undeniable proof that Scallion's predictions are coming true.

Scallion predicted the course of Hurricane Andrew in 1992 with an astonishing level of accuracy.

CHAPTER 5

CURSES

Curses are a form of magic spell uttered with the intention of harming a person or place. Over time, vast numbers of curses have been passed, fuelling superstition around these unseen and inexplicable forces. Many who scorn the idea of a curse nevertheless have a lucky mascot on their desks when they sit their examinations. Like the talismans of our ancestors, they are believed to bestow magical powers on the wearer and protect against misfortune. Whether or not curses can truly affect us, their power will remain as long as people continue to believe in them.

THE POWER OF CURSES

Can the utterance of a few malicious words really change someone's destiny? Those who believe in the power of a curse are convinced that catastrophe will follow in its wake. And sometimes ensuing mishaps and disasters are so bizarre and numerous that all the evidence points to a jinx.

CURSE OF THE BOY KING

Perhaps the most infamous curse of all was one that protected the tomb of King Tutankhamen. When Egyptologist Howard Carter discovered the tomb in 1922, it was the culmination of a career spent scouring the desert for riches. The honour of opening the inner

Lord Carnarvon and Howard Carter with Carnarvon's daughter, Lady Evelyn Herbert, at the entrance to the tomb of Tutankhamen.

door, revealing the treasures of the king in all their splendour, fell to Lord Carnarvon (financier of the expedition) on 17 February 1923. Within weeks after that fateful day Carnarvon was dead, apparently from an infected mosquito bite. The bite mark on his cheek was said to resemble one borne by the boy king himself.

When Carnarvon died, the lights in Cairo flickered and failed, while miles away at home his dog fell into a fit and passed away. Tales of other expedition members dying suddenly abounded. Even the pilots who took the royal artifacts as cargo on their planes apparently met unexpected deaths. For several years the string of ill fortune continued, as museum curators associated with the exhibition of Tutankhamen's treasures keeled over.

The curse that protected the tomb was written in hieroglyphics on a clay tablet. When deciphered, it read: 'Death will slay with its wings whoever disturbs the peace of the Pharaoh.' Yet, despite careful cataloguing of all the tomb's contents, the dire warning has vanished. Perhaps it never existed in the first place, being the product of some sun-affected imagination. However, there is another explanation. Carter may well have hidden the tablet bearing the curse to prevent a walk-out by superstitious local workers, on whom he was reliant for his work. Cynics have poured scorn over the curse claims, pointing out that mosquito bites were and still are frequently fatal. They say that the lights in Cairo often blacked out, and that the story of the death of Carnarvon's dog is only anecdotal. Much has recently been made of the theory that the tomb contained lethal spores that afflicted those who went inside, giving weight to the sceptics' argument. Yet when Carter died a decade later it was from natural causes. The debate on the curse continues.

Unluckiest of all, of course, was King Tutankhamen himself, who died when he was still a teenager and whose memorial was all but erased by subsequent royals.

Tutankhamen's gold burial mask. The death of Lord Carnarvon shortly after entering the tomb.

A HISTORY OF CURSES

Belief in curses stretches back into the mists of time. Ancient verbal curses may seem comical today, but in the past they would strike terror into the heart: 'May the seven terriers of hell sit on the spool of your breast and bark in at your soulcase,' says an old Irish curse. 'She should have stones and not children,' according to a Yiddish one.

In the past people have made a profitable business out of issuing curses. The philosopher Plato (427–347BC) wrote in *The Republic*, 'If anyone wishes to injure an enemy; for a small fee they (sorcerers) will bring harm on good or bad alike, binding the gods to serve their purposes by spells and curses.' Curses are a common Biblical theme, perhaps the most famous being issued by God against Adam and Eve in the Garden of Eden.

THE HOPE DIAMOND

A wrathful god appears to have orchestrated fearful vengeance after the Hope diamond was plundered from a temple in Mandala, Burma in the 17th century. Mined in India, it was a fabulous violet-coloured specimen of the very highest quality. No one knows what happened to the thief, but it fell into the possession of a French trader, Jean-Baptiste Tavernier. Tavernier sold the diamond to French king Louis XIV, who had it made into a heart before giving it to his mistress Madame de Montespan. Shortly afterwards she was publicly disgraced in a black magic scandal. The luckless trader Tavernier met a grisly end on a trip to Russia and dogs were discovered gnawing on his bones.

The gem remained in the royal collection, and it was worn by Marie Antoinette before she was beheaded in the French Revolution. In the chaos that enveloped Paris it was stolen and its whereabouts were unknown for some three decades. Could it be that the curse of the Hope Diamond had finally lost its power?

LIVES DESTROYED

The diamond turned up in the 1830s, in the possession of Dutch diamond cutter Wilhelm Fals. Its exquisite beauty bewitched his son Hendrick, and the hapless boy ultimately committed suicide. The dangerous gem was then bought by the banker Henry Philip Hope, who gave it his name, but suffered no harm from it. Afterwards, though, the curse appears to have gained some momentum. It was bequeathed to a relative, Lord Francis Hope, whose marriage collapsed. By 1904 a certain Jacques Colot was the owner, until he lost his mind and committed suicide. Russian nobleman Prince Kanilovsky presented it to his lover, whom he later shot and killed before being bludgeoned to death himself. Diamond dealer Habib Bey drowned and Greek merchant Simon Montharides plunged to his death with his wife and child when their horse and carriage went over a cliff top. The Hope diamond then went to the Ottoman ruler, Abdul Hamid III, shortly before an uprising usurped the Sultanate. His favourite wife, often seen wearing the jewel, was stabbed to death.

> 'What tragedies have befallen me might have occurred had I never seen or touched the Hope Diamond. My observations have persuaded me that tragedies, for anyone who lives, are not escapable.'
>
> Evelyn Walsh McLean

LAST REVENGE

The last ill-fated owner was wealthy Evelyn Walsh McLean. Within a year of purchasing the diamond from jewellery impresario Pierre Cartier for $180,000, her son Vinson was killed in a car accident. Her husband Ned began drinking, left her for another woman and finally lost his mind. Then, in 1946, their daughter took an overdose of sleeping pills. After Evelyn died in 1947 the gem finally went into the Smithsonian Institute in Washington, a move that appears to have neutered its potency. Evelyn had received numerous warnings about the curse of the Hope diamond, many in unsolicited letters from strangers. But she maintained that the bad luck attached to its ownership was pure chance. 'What tragedies have befallen me might have occurred had I never seen or touched the Hope Diamond. My observations have persuaded me that tragedies, for anyone who lives, are not escapable.'

From treading the sacred corridors of Tutankhamen's tomb, to plundering the exquisite jewels of Burma, many of the most potent curses seem to be released when humans tread too far into forbidden territory. And where some curses seem to lose potency over time, others retain their venom, wreaking havoc down hapless generations...

Evelyn Walsh McLean, who bought the Hope diamond from jewellery impresario Pierre Cartier for $180,000.

HAITIAN ZOMBIES

We think of zombies as the dreadful, decomposing creatures with a taste for human flesh that we see in films. These are, of course, the products of fertile imaginations and talented make-up artists in the film studios. Yet there is evidence to show that zombies really do exist. Sapped of their personalities, probably by a cocktail of drugs, they are lowly slaves rendered incapable of independent action.

The phenomenon of zombies is associated with the voodoo faith in Haiti, and there are several well-documented examples, including that of Clairvius Narcisse. Clairvius Narcisse died at the Albert Schweitzer Hospital in Haiti in 1962. After his death had been certified, he was buried. Eighteen years later, Clairvius himself turned up at his sister's house, very much alive, and able to recount stories from their childhood that only he could know. He told how his brothers had been angry about his refusal to sell family land, and how they had sought revenge by ordering his zombification.

After his burial, during which he lay conscious but inert in his coffin, Clairvius was taken from the graveyard and became the subject of spells by a voodoo witch doctor (known as a bokor) that turned him into an 'empty vessel'. He was able to move, but he could not communicate properly and had lost his free will. Voodoo worshippers see a zombie as a body without a soul, and this is what he seemed to have become. For two years he worked in the fields alongside other zombies. After the death of his master he lived rough for 18 years, returning home only when he was sure that the brothers who engineered his zombification were themselves dead.

Clairius' story matched with the hospital records. His cheek bore a scar that, he said, was inflicted when

> 'Zombiism actually exists. There are Haitians who have been raised from their graves and returned to life.'
>
> Dr E. Wade Davis

Felicia Felix-Mentor from Haiti, who died and was buried in 1907. She was found wandering about the countryside in a zombified state in 1937.

a nail was driven into his coffin. So just what happened to him after his 'death' in hospital?

For years the assumption was that zombies – if they existed – were literally raised from the dead through the supernatural powers of the bokor. Today it seems more likely that a poison is administered to a living victim. This poison slows down bodily functions so much that they become imperceptible and the body seems corpse-like. Following burial, the barely-breathing body is then retrieved and further drugs are given that bring about a controlled recovery. So while the victim might regain physical strength, his mind remains feeble, his memory is all but erased and he is effectively powerless.

Much of the mystery was revealed by anthropologist Dr E. Wade Davis, who, following extensive research, assured the world that zombiism was a real phenomenon.

Davis analysed some of the poisons used by bokors and found toad skin and puffer fish were two of the most significant ingredients in the poison used to induce a coma. Toad venom is known as a potent painkiller, while the puffer fish contains tetrodotoxin that affects the nervous system. Thereafter, different drugs, including Jimson's Weed (a poisonous type of nightshade plant), are used to keep the victims of zombification stupefied.

Davis acknowledges that the deep religious beliefs prevailing in Haiti are vital to the process carried out by the bokor. Because people believe in zombiism, it is more likely to become a reality. The voodoo religion is intense and ritualistic, although not inevitably sinister. Broadly speaking, voodoo is a cross between native African beliefs and the Catholic faith once forced upon slaves when they were transported to destinations like Haiti. Davis believes that zombiism is carried out as a punishment and the mindset of the Haitian people permits bokors to do their worst.

Some commentators remain unconvinced, and question whether zombies exist at all. One piece of research found that the vast majority of Haitians said they knew of a zombie. On further examination, however, it was always a distant cousin or friend of a friend that was the zombie rather than someone they knew well. Another theory is that the zombies are in fact people suffering from mental illness who, in the absence of an effective healthcare system, are compelled to wander the countryside begging or undertaking menial labouring jobs to survive. Bereaved relatives identify the so-called zombies as family members through the distortion of grief and because of a desire to see the dead person once more.

The toxins in puffer fish are a significant ingredient in the poisons used by bokors. A delicacy in Japan, where it is enjoyed for making taste-buds tingle, the fish has induced coma and even death in some diners.

THE LITTLE

James Dean, the iconic Hollywood film star, died tragically young, at a point in his life when his acting career was going from strength to strength. Although he had starred in only a few films, he had earned himself much acclaim and a sizeable fortune.

With his new-found riches, Dean had bought a sports car, a Porsche Spyder, one of only 90 in the world at that time. He nicknamed the car 'The Little Bastard', and had this name painted on the machine along with a racing stripe.

Dean had intended to race his beloved car himself, but sadly never had the chance. On 30 September 1955, only two weeks after he had bought the car, he died in

BASTARD

it, following a head-on collision with another vehicle. The driver of the other car survived, having sustained only cuts and bruises.

In the weeks preceding his death, Dean had been seen driving his car everywhere, proudly displaying it to all of his friends, although he was surprised to find that many of them failed to share his enthusiasm for the powerful machine.

Several of them apparently felt a sense of horror when they saw the vehicle – some out of concern for the dangers that such a fast car might pose to Dean's reckless nature, others simply because of an innate sense of foreboding about the machine.

At the time, Dean would not have been aware that a number of strange happenings had already been linked with the car since its arrival at the Competition Motors showroom. Several mechanics had hurt themselves on the car shortly after it was delivered, one breaking his thumb after trapping it in one of the doors and another cutting himself as he adjusted the engine. At the time, these events seemed to be no more than accidents, but later they would be seen as part of a much larger pattern of misfortune, or even something altogether more sinister.

After the fatal crash, the car wreckage was bought for salvage by the motor mechanic George Barris, the

James Dean, the iconic Hollywood star who died aged only 24.

very man who had customized the machine for Dean several weeks earlier. It was only when he began to re-use parts of the car that he started to suspect that some form of terrible curse might be attached to the vehicle, a curse that had not only claimed the life of the young film star, but was also causing numerous other disasters in the lives of those unlucky enough to have acquired a piece of the car.

The engine of 'The Little Bastard' had been largely undamaged by the crash, so Barris had reconditioned it and sold it to a racing enthusiast, Dr William F. Eschrich.

One of the doctor's friends and fellow racer, Dr Carl McHenry, learned of the sale and decided to buy the transaxle of the car. Barris also sold several other vehicle parts, including the two back tyres.

In the first race in which the two doctors tested their new equipment, both men were involved in serious accidents. Dr Eschrich's car turned over after locking up on entering a bend. Fortunately he survived the crash, although he was left paralyzed. Dr McHenry was not so lucky: he was killed after losing control of the car and hitting a tree. As if this were not enough, before the week was out, the driver who had bought the two back tyres narrowly escaped death after both tyres blew out simultaneously during another race.

Learning of the multiple disasters, Barris decided that he would try to put the car to some kind of beneficial use. Accordingly, he lent the crumpled machine to the California Highway Safety Patrol for publicity purposes, thinking that Dean's fame would greatly enhance their campaign on accident prevention. Unfortunately, at that point he did not realize that the car was actually a source of accidents in itself.

The car was taken into the possession of the Highway Patrol and stored in a garage with a large number of other cars. While it was there, a mysterious fire broke out – many cars were completely destroyed and almost all incurred serious damage. Curiously, 'The Little Bastard' emerged from the fire remarkably unscathed.

A short time later, while the car was being taken to

Dean with his beloved Porsche 550 Spyder, in which he suffered his fatal accident. Even after the crash, the car continued to cause trouble – accidents continued to follow it as the intact engine was transferred to another car.

a display area for demonstration purposes, a strange accident took place. Dean's car was being transported on the back of a flat-bed truck, driven by an experienced driver named George Barhuis, when it skidded on a wet road, and the truck's rig crashed into a ditch. Barhuis was thrown from the cab by the impact, but is believed to have survived the crash. However, in a bewildering tragedy, he was then killed when the wreck of 'The Little Bastard' fell from the back of the truck and landed on top of him, crushing him to death.

Yet the litany of disasters was still not complete. On the fourth anniversary of Dean's fatal crash, a teenager in Detroit was viewing the car, which was on a large display stand. Without warning, the structure on which the car was resting collapsed, and the car toppled forward crushing the boy's legs. It seems inconceivable that, following this, the car was still put out on display to the public.

A few weeks after this accident, the car was once again being transported by truck, when it fell from the back of the vehicle, smashing into the road and causing the serious injury of yet more people.

Fortunately, the cursed car was doomed itself. Shortly after this final accident, the vehicle spontaneously fell apart while on show in New Orleans. Attempts were made to put it back together, but George Barris stepped in and arranged to have the remains of the car transported back to his garage in California. When the delivery arrived, the container was opened and, to their astonishment, the car had disappeared.

It is not known if it had been stolen by an obsessive admirer of the film star, but no trace of it has ever been found. Certainly, if anyone had been foolish enough to take the vehicle into their own possession, they would have been very fortunate to escape the curse that had randomly struck at those connected with the car. Nevertheless, the fact that it is now missing can only add to the sense of mystery that surrounds not only this jinxed machine, but also the tragic, doomed figure of James Dean.

The grave of James Dean in Fairmount, Indiana. His life was cut tragically short due to a car accident.

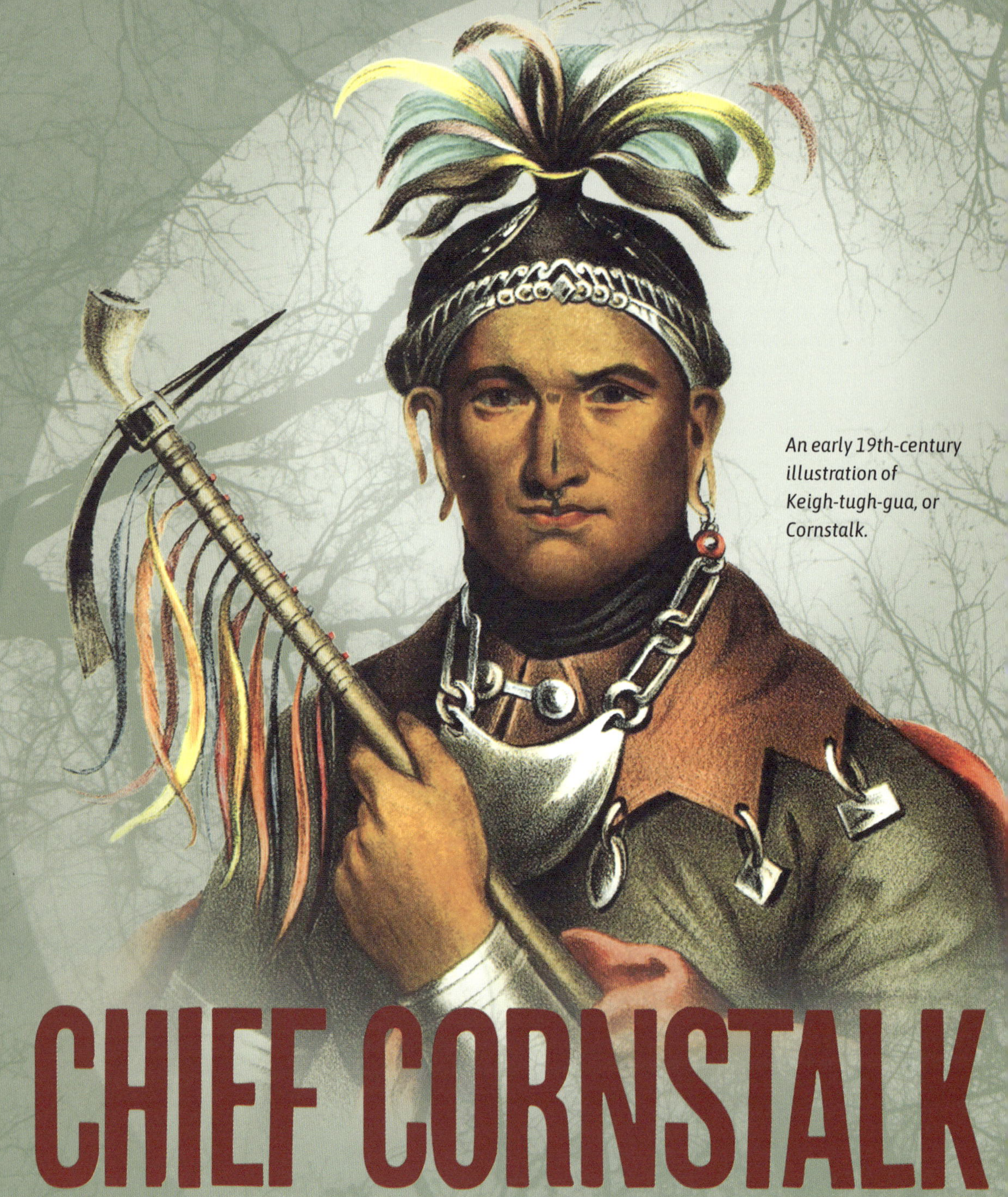

An early 19th-century illustration of Keigh-tugh-gua, or Cornstalk.

CHIEF CORNSTALK

For many years the area of West Virginia known as Point Pleasant has been beset by disasters and misfortunes. Although these could be attributed to nothing more than bad luck, some ascribe the events to the ancient curse of a betrayed Native American chief.

In order to understand the nature and power of a curse, it is necessary to know the background to the events – only then can it be judged whether there could have been sufficient cause for such a potent force of revenge. The story in this particular case dates back more than 200 years, to the 1770s, when the American frontiersmen were battling against the Native Americans in their attempts to push west, and later fighting the British for their independence.

As the American settlers found their way to the land around the Ohio River, now West Virginia, they encountered strong resistance from the Native American tribes, some of whom had joined together to form a powerful confederacy. This was led by the chieftain of the Shawnee tribe, a man called Keigh-tugh-gua (Cornstalk).

A battle between the American settlers and the Native Americans took place in 1774, and both sides sustained heavy losses. The Native Americans were forced to retreat westwards as the settlers took over the land and fortified it. Cornstalk, recognizing that he would have trouble defeating such heavily armed men, decided to make peace with them.

A few years later, trouble was to erupt again, as the British began to stir up feeling against the rebellious settlers. They tried to bring as many Native Americans on to their side as possible and several tribes from Cornstalk's old confederacy joined them to prepare an attack on the settlements. Cornstalk chose instead to honour his peace and he and another chief, Red Hawk of the Delaware tribe, went to the American fort to discuss the situation.

On their arrival, the chieftains were taken hostage by the Americans, as it was believed that the Native Americans would not attack while their chiefs were being held. While in captivity, Cornstalk was well treated, and even assisted the American settlers in planning their tactics against the British. After a few days, Cornstalk's young son, Ellinipisco, came to the fort with news for his father, whereupon he was also taken hostage.

'I came to this fort as your friend and you murdered me. You have murdered by my side my young son. For this may the curse of the Great Spirit rest upon this land. May it be blighted by nature. May it be blighted in its hopes.'

Shortly after this, events took a dramatic turn for the worse after a number of American soldiers who had gone out to hunt deer were ambushed and killed by Native Americans. When this was discovered, discipline inside the fort broke down and an angry mob broke into the prisoners' quarters with murder in mind. They showed no mercy to Cornstalk or his young son, who was shot before his very eyes. It was this act of murder and betrayal that prompted Cornstalk to utter his mighty

A reconstruction of Fort Randolph, Point Pleasant, where Chief Cornstalk was murdered.

The gravesite of Chief Cornstalk at Point Pleasant, West Virginia.

curse, words that, it seems, have affected the area for hundreds of years.

After these tragic events had taken place, Cornstalk was afforded a proper burial, and he was interred near the fort where he had been killed. He was not allowed to rest in peace, however, since his remains were dug up and moved twice for the sake of new buildings and monuments – first in 1840, and then again in 1950. If the original act of betrayal had not been sufficient to secure the power of the curse, then the desecration of his grave surely was.

This area became known as Point Pleasant and, almost in defiance of the curse, residents decided to erect a monument in honour of the soldiers who had defeated Cornstalk in the first battle of 1774. Strangely, this monument was to be struck twice by lightning, first in 1909, delaying its unveiling ceremony, and then again in 1921, causing serious damage.

These happenings were nothing, however, compared to the catalogue of disasters that was to befall this relatively small community. In 1880 a huge fire ravaged an entire block in the centre of town, while in 1907 America's worst mining disaster was responsible for the deaths of 310 men. In 1967, the Silver Bridge disaster killed 46 people. This coincided with strange local sightings such as lights in the sky and the regular appearance of the mysterious stalker known as 'Mothman'.

Shortly after this, in 1968 and 1970, a number of aircraft crashed in the area, killing more than 100 passengers. In 1978 a derailed freight train caused an immense spill of toxic chemicals that poisoned that land and the water basin of the area, destroying all the local wells.

It is thought that this environmental catastrophe could be the blight of nature mentioned in Cornstalk's curse, while the blighting of hope appears to have been manifest in the depressed economy of Point Pleasant.

There are many who would maintain that when disaster befalls a person or community, it is just a matter of misfortune. To suggest that it is as a result of a curse, they say, is to resort to ancient superstitions which have no place in the modern world. When, however, such a huge chain of catastrophes occurs, as has been the case with Point Pleasant, it is difficult not to admit that a curse might have been responsible after all.

The Mothman statue at Point Pleasant, West Virginia. By the mid-1960s, reportings of the 'Mothman' were widespread in the area.

THE BLACK HOPE CURSE

The Haneys built their house on top of a forgotten cemetery named Black Hope.

Some curses are so general that they are feared by large numbers of people or entire populations. Trinkets and lucky charms are often worn as a means of self-protection. Other curses are more specific, directed at a particular person, group or place – often these individual stories become woven into the very fabric of superstition, reinforcing the notion that such malevolent powers do, in fact, exist.

This type of personal experience was certainly the case as far as the Haney and Williams families were concerned, when they bought their brand-new homes near Houston, Texas, in 1982. Moving into the neighbourhood was the culmination of their family dreams, as their houses were set in large gardens on an attractive new estate.

One year after the move, Sam and Judith Haney appeared to have settled well into their new home. This was all to change, however, when they decided to have a swimming pool built in their garden. Digging commenced, whereupon an elderly man living in the area knocked on their door and brought them some unsettling news.

He informed them that their new house was built on the site of an old African-American burial ground and that, in excavating part of the garden for the swimming pool, they were digging precisely over some of the graves. He even gave the Haneys the names of some black families who used to live in the area so that they could corroborate his story. The Haneys, however, were sceptical and continued work on the pool.

After a short while, two crude coffins were unearthed, containing the remains of a man and a woman. Appalled by their discovery, the Haneys realized that the old man had been right. Once the shock had settled, they decided that it was imperative that the bodies should be returned to their resting place with a proper burial.

So they set about trying to establish the identity of the bodies. Their search culminated in the discovery of an elderly man, Jasper Norton, who had worked as a gravedigger within the former black community. He informed the Haneys that the housing estate on which they lived was indeed built on the site of a former cemetery which had been named Black Hope, and contained mainly the graves of slaves. He identified the exhumed bodies as belonging to two slaves, Charlie and Betty Thomas, who had died when he was a young man.

The Haneys continued their search, this time for descendants of the buried couple. When this proved fruitless, they decided to return the remains to the spot from which they had come. They were troubled at

During the construction of a swimming pool for their house, the Haneys unearthed coffins containing human remains – it was not long before they began encountering supernatural disturbances.

having disturbed a grave, and hoped that, by reburial, they could lay the whole episode to rest – as events were to reveal, however, they were very much mistaken.

Not long after they had reburied the bodies, the Haneys' lives began to be affected by strange happenings. At first, this took the form of disembodied voices that disturbed their nightly sleep, but soon there were other incidents such as appliances and lights spontaneously turning on and off, further unnatural noises and the discovery of a pair of Judith Haney's shoes on the very spot where Betty Thomas lay buried.

After a while, the Haneys' fear and bewilderment grew to such an extent that they confided in their neighbours, Ben and Jean Williams. To their amazement, they discovered that they were not the only family to have suffered from paranormal interventions – at least a dozen of the households had experienced some kind of unexplained activity, ranging from doors opening and closing to strange apparitions.

Like the Haneys, the Williams family also believed that they were being persecuted by a curse from beyond the grave. Although they had not themselves actually found any corpses on their land, they had been astonished to find that nothing seemed to grow in their garden, and that strange, deep holes would continually appear, forming afresh even after they had been filled in. This belief turned to outright conviction when six members of the Williams family were diagnosed with cancer in the same year – sadly, for three of them, this was fatal. As far as the Williams were concerned, this was a direct intervention from beyond the grave.

Events took an even more tragic turn when Jean Williams decided to find out whether there were any graves in her garden, such as there were on the

Haneys' land. So one day she and her daughter, Tina, started to dig up the garden. After a short while, Tina collapsed. Two days later, she died from a heart attack, aged just 30.

Could it be that these two families were right and that the dead had objected so strongly to the desecration of their graves that they had managed to bridge the gap between their world and ours? For the residents of the former Black Hope cemetery, there was no question. They believed that the land was cursed, and that they had activated this curse by disturbing the graves.

Events proved too much for the Haney and Williams families, who decided to sell up and move on. Whatever force had been acting upon them, whether it was the workings of their own subconscious or the 'Black Hope Curse' itself, several lives had been lost and many families had been driven from their homes in fear.

Curiously, subsequent tenants of their former homes did not report any problems at all. Had the spirits' anger been satisfied, or had the unpleasant knowledge that they lived above a graveyard just been too much for the 'cursed' families? If events had been restricted solely to the occasional strange happening within the households, then perhaps they could have been accused of paranoia. The extent of the illnesses and deaths involved, however, seem to make the case for a curse a rather convincing one.

Was the knowledge of living above a burial ground too much for the inhabitants, or was there a real curse at work?

THE EARLS OF MAR

The ruins of Alloa Tower in Scotland are now all that remains of a vast manor, the hereditary seat of the Erskine family, the Earls of Mar. The fate of the place was interwoven with that of the family who lived there, not just because they had lived there for generations, but because of the curse that predicted and assured the doom of the family and the seat of their power.

It is believed that this curse was uttered against the Earl of Mar by the Abbot of Cambuskenneth during the 16th century. In destroying the Abbey at Cambuskenneth, the Earl had unwittingly sealed the fate of his lineage for years to come, for many of the predicted details of the curse, although cryptic when uttered, were to come shockingly true.

Remarkably, it was not unusual at that time for Scottish curses to predict suffering that would last for several generations, but this particular curse was very specific about certain matters. Most importantly, and typically for a curse of this kind, it was foretold that the Erskine family would become extinct – a fate which was the ultimate disaster for any hereditary aristocratic lineage. The curse elaborated further: before the family died out, all its estates and property would fall into the hands of strangers – again, this would have been a horrifying concept to a family of landed gentry.

At this point, it might have been expected that even the Abbot's rage would have been satisfied, but the curse continued.

It predicted that a future Erskine would later live to see his home consumed by flames while his wife burned inside it and three of his children would never see the light of day. Moreover, adding further disgrace to the name of Erksine, the great hall of the family seat would be used to stable horses and a lowly weaver would work in the grand chamber of state. The curse was predicted to end only after all this had passed and an ash sapling had taken root at the top of the tower. Although the curse must have worried the Earl of Mar, he managed to live his entire life without seeing any of the predicted events come true and, on his deathbed, he must have reflected that the family had escaped from the Abbot's wrathful utterings. In this, he was greatly mistaken.

This seems to have been a patient curse because it was a while before certain events began to show the

The curse was cast on John Erskine, the 1st Earl of Mar, and his descendants.

The remains of Cambuskenneth Abbey, after it was destroyed by the Earl of Mar in the mid-16th century.

The Earl of Mar leads the Jacobite Rising of 1715. Its failure led to the loss of his land and titles.

truth behind the predictions. In 1715, a subsequent Earl of Mar declared his allegiance to James Stuart, the son of James VII of Scotland, who was known as 'the Old Pretender'. The Earl led a failed Jacobite rebellion against the crown in an attempt to install James Stuart as king. He was defeated and, in retribution, the family were stripped of their land and titles – in this way, one part of the curse had come true. Whether the Earl actually attributed this to the curse is unknown, as he might have merely viewed events as a punishment for his own actions. However, more of the predictions were to be borne out within a few generations.

Almost a century later, in 1801, it was John Francis Erskine who was unlucky enough to bear the brunt of the prophecy, and so pay the price for his ancestor's mistakes. To begin with, three of his children were born completely blind – thus, as the curse had foretold, they would 'never see the light of day'. Then Alloa Tower, all that remained of the family's former glory, was devastated by fire and Erskine's wife perished in the flames.

The main body of the curse had now come true and only the details were left to be completed. Sure enough, a troop of cavalry used the half-ruined hall as shelter for their horses while they were moving around the country. Subsequently, a homeless weaver took up residence in the ruins of the building and plied his trade in the nearby town. In around 1820 a small ash tree was seen to have taken root in the ruins of Alloa Tower. The curse had now been fulfilled in every detail.

Of all the questions that spring to mind in this case, the first revolves around the existence of the curse. Was it ever really uttered or could it have been made up after the events to explain and justify the

Alloa Tower, the seat of the Earls of Mar.

demise of the Erskines and serve as a useful warning to other potentially rebellious landowners? Certainly, both historical fact and local folklore indicate that the curse was true, but there is always the possibility that, rather than having the ability to bring about such terrible events, the Abbot was simply in possession of astonishing visionary powers.

Either possibility could apply in this case. Perhaps the Abbot did have the power to seal the destiny of the Erskine family through a curse, or maybe his powers of divination were comparable to those of a prophet, although this would appear to be the only instance of such a prediction from the Abbot. Whatever the truth of the matter, it seems that the mystical powers of the Abbot of Cambuskenneth were so great that they are remembered to this very day.

The coat of arms of the Earldom of Mar.

CHAPTER 6

CREATURES OF MYSTERY

Could there really be supernatural or malevolent beasts roaming the furthest reaches of the planet, occasionally emerging to terrify witnesses? Without photos, film footage or a corpse, there is no firm proof that such creatures exist. But anecdotal evidence is compelling and cryptozoology – the study of unknown species – is a burgeoning branch of science. Perhaps it is only a matter of time before we will be forced to change our minds.

The Earth's oceans are huge, unexplored underground kingdoms that have held mankind in their thrall for thousands of years. Today, these inaccessible areas remain as mysterious as the infinite expanses of space, although scientific advances have recently attempted to push back the boundaries of sub-aquatic understanding in order to cast some light on the black depths that cover our planet. This has produced several surprising results.

Scientists have established that one of the most effective methods of obtaining information about the underwater world is through the use of hydrophones. The origins of these underwater microphones can be traced back to the 1960s when they were utilized widely by the US Navy for the purpose of detecting the presence of Soviet submarines during the Cold War. Today, they have been found to be ideal for tracing, tracking and identifying the many sounds travelling through the water.

SOUNDS OF THE DEEP

The hydrophones, which are in essence a kind of listening station, are positioned hundreds of metres below the ocean surface. At this depth, factors such as pressure and temperature trap the sound waves within a layer known as the depth sound channel and, as a consequence, the waves travel for many thousands of kilometres without suffering distortion.

When the sound waves come into contact with hydrophones they produce a spectrogram, a visual representation of sound. This can be analysed and compared to other, known, spectrogram patterns. Many ocean noises – such as those made by boats, submarines, whales and earth tremors, for example – occur frequently and are easily identifiable in this way, but there remains a large number of eerie echoes that evade explanation.

Most of these inexplicable noises occur at a low frequency and, therefore, have to be speeded up in order to be rendered audible to the human ear. While some sounds last for just a few minutes, others continue for years at a time, baffling researchers. Although underground volcanoes, icebergs and even enormous, undiscovered animals residing within the ocean depths have all been suggested as possible reasons for these peculiar sounds, the truth is still unknown.

One particularly mysterious noise picked up by hydrophone has been nicknamed 'Bloop'. While scientists suspect that this strange sound may emanate from an animal, since the spectrogram pattern showed the rapid variation in frequency characteristic of that produced by deep-sea creatures, there is one surprising factor in this case – the sheer volume of the noise.

The fact that the Bloop signal has been detected simultaneously by sensors located more than 4,800km (2,592 nautical miles) apart indicates that the noise produced is louder than that caused by any known animal. It has been suggested, therefore, that a giant squid, or some other type of undiscovered monster, could be roaming the depths of our oceans.

'Slowdown' is the name given to another signal that, again, raises more questions than it answers. The sound has been detected in the Pacific and Atlantic oceans several times a year since 1997, and continues to

baffle experts all over the world. One leading scientist, Christopher Fox, observed that the noise, which he likened to that of an aircraft, was coming from a southerly direction and so may have originated in the Antarctic. In order to rule out any obvious, man-made explanation, he consulted the US Navy. His suspicions that the sound could have been caused by top-secret military equipment were, however, unfounded.

Another theory which is currently being studied is that the noise could be caused by the shifting of Antarctic ice at the South Pole. The spectrogram pattern produced by Slowdown is similar to that created in cases where friction is a factor, and might have arisen in this instance from the moving and shifting of huge masses of ice over land.

Many further tests will be necessary before the true origin of sounds such as Bloop and Slowdown can be confirmed. Whether they are indeed caused by the movements of mysterious alien creatures in the underwater depths, or whether there are other – purely geological – explanations, only time will tell.

A hydrophone is launched into the ocean. Situated hundreds of metres below the surface, they can detect all manner of underwater sounds.

The Kraken was said to have flailing arms or tentacles that could reach as high as the top of a ship's mast.

KRAKEN

Sailors have long believed that gruesome beasts with a taste for blood lurk beneath the waves, occasionally surfacing to attack a passing ship and its unfortunate crew. On land, people have been swift to dismiss their tales as ludicrous exaggeration. But the latest scientific evidence says that they were right to be fearful of mighty creatures from the deep.

The monster most feared by sailors down the centuries was known as the Kraken. Its flailing arms reached as high as the lookout nests in the masts of sailing ships, it had eyes the size of footballs and it was commonly depicted with the dimensions of a small island. Probably seen over 2,000 years ago in classical times, the Kraken has been variously described as a squid, an octopus, a whale, a crab and a lobster.

Persuasive records of the Kraken exist in the *Speculum Regale*, or *King's Mirror*, a Scandinavian text in the form of a conversation between a father and son dating from 1250.

Over the course of many years, the remains of huge sea beasts have been washed ashore, and the rotting residue of tentacled creatures has been discovered in the stomachs of whales. More recently, entire, smaller, juvenile specimens of these mysterious squid have been caught in deep-sea trawlers and brought to the Institute for Antarctic and Southern Ocean Studies in Tasmania, for examination.

Speculation about a hitherto unidentified underwater beast was fuelled when a partly decayed body was discovered on a Florida beach in 1896. The body was 5.5m (18ft) long and some 3m (10ft) wide. Detached tentacles were in the order of 11m (36ft) in length. Local naturalist De Witt Webb was sure it was an octopus, although other experts believed it could have been the remains of a whale.

But an octopus, even one of gigantic proportions, tends to be a shy creature and would be unlikely to attack ships. His cephalopod cousin the squid, with ten rather than eight tentacles, is far more aggressive and seems a more convincing candidate for Kraken.

Two particular types of squid are in the frame but, until a short time ago, evidence for both was in short supply. Until recently, mystery cloaked the activities of the giant squid (Architeutis dux), thanks to its secretive nature. This tentacled sea monster was identified back in 1856 by a Danish researcher. The best indicator scientists had of its existence was the presence of a few tentacles in the stomach of predator whales. In 2001 a body was discovered off the coast of Spain, spurring scientists on to make fresh calculations about its lifestyle. It is believed that giant squid can reach up

37

'I can say nothing definite as to its length...for on those occasions when men have seen it, it has appeared more like an island than a fish. Nor have I heard that one has ever been caught or found dead. It seems likely that there are but two in all the ocean and that these beget no offspring, for I believe it is always the same ones that appear.'

to 18m (59ft) in length and that their daily diet typically consists of 50kg (110lb) of fish.

Despite all the horror stories about the creature's ferocity, however, recent studies have concluded that, despite its mammoth proportions, it is in fact very slow and relatively weak. It is thought to drift in the cold currents of the deep ocean rather than dart to attack its prey, and its pincer action is believed to be clumsy and feeble.

Numerous questions about this giant squid have yet to be answered. For example, how many different populations exist in the oceans of the world? How long do these creatures live? What do they eat and how often? How many years do they take to reach maturity?

As far as the last question is concerned, it seems reasonable to assume that, in view of the animal's great size, the growth period is considerable. However, studies of other squid have revealed otherwise, and some people actually believe that the total time taken to reach maturity could be as little as two years. This would make the creature one of the fastest growing beasts in the entire animal kingdom. Scientists are working hard to try to understand more about this enormous sea-dweller, and in so doing, hope to be able to shed light on other species of giant squid at the same time.

Another species in which researchers are particularly interested is the Mesonychoteuthis or 'colossal squid'. Rumours about this variety of squid, which is thought to be even larger than Architeuthis, have been rife since 1925, when two tentacles were found in the stomach of a sperm whale. In 2004 the juvenile body of one of these creatures was caught off Antarctica. From studies carried out on the corpse, scientists have estimated that, had it reached maturity, it would have measured an astounding 15m (49ft) in length.

YEAR OF THE SQUID

2003 proved a pivotal year for squid-watchers. In January of that year, a French yacht taking part in the round-the-world race for the Jules Verne Trophy became enveloped in the arms of a giant squid. Yachtsman Olivier De Kersauson realized the creature was clamped to his boat's hull when he caught sight of a tentacle through a porthole.

'It was thicker than my leg and it was really pulling the boat hard,' said De Kersauson, who was close to the Portuguese island of Madeira when the incident happened. The squid, measuring an estimated 8.5m (28ft) in length, was jamming the rudder of the boat, effectively putting the vessel out of action. Giant squid can exert an amazing amount of strength by using the visible flaps of muscle at the top of their tentacles. The suckers that help them to cling onto boats and other surfaces are the size of dinner plates. Fortunately for De Kersauson and his crew, the squid released its grip when the vessel stopped. 'We didn't have anything to scare off this beast, so I don't know what we would have done if it hadn't let go,' Mr De Kersauson said. 'We weren't going to attack it with our penknives. I've never seen anything like it in 40 years of sailing.'

De Kerauson was one step ahead of marine scientists, who have never yet seen a giant squid alive. But, more significantly still, in April that year a colossal squid (Mesonychoteuthis hamiltoni) was retrieved almost intact from the Ross Sea in the Antarctic. Although it was dead, it gave scientists their first opportunity to study the species, which was first officially identified in 1925.

Its overall length could not be calculated due to tentacle damage, but its mantle (body) measured 2.3m (8ft), already exceeding the maximum body length of the giant squid. Startlingly, scientists believed it was not yet fully grown. One feature that set it apart from other squid were swivelling hooks on the clubs at the end of its barbed tentacles. It also has the largest beak of all known squid. Both the giant and colossal squid stay well away from mankind at depths of between 60m (197ft) and 300m (984ft) in cold waters. Evidence of their sinister strength has been found on the washed up bodies of mighty sperm whales that appear to have sustained deep cuts following squid attacks.

A model of Architeuthis on display in the Natural History Museum in London. The model was destroyed in 1940 during World War II after a bomb hit the gallery.

It would seem that this species is responsible for all the terrifying tales about tentacled sea monsters. The colossal squid is physiologically different from its feeble, drifting cousin, the Architeuthis, being armed and deadly. It possesses a powerful, muscular fin, and has rotating hooks along its arms and tentacles. These factors would seem to correlate with the scars and sucker wounds found on the whales that share the freezing habitat of this creature, which is thought to be capable of striking with speed and lethal accuracy.

Many of these postulations are based on theory and on the studies of other species of squid. From the work carried out, scientists now believe that the colossal squid is not only the biggest invertebrate known to mankind but also one of the most aggressive predators on earth. Unexpectedly, their assertions have given credence to the stories of sailors from a bygone age.

A giant squid in the sea. It is likely that such creatures formed the basis for the legends of the kraken.

LAKE MONSTERS

Many stories exist of serpent-like monsters living in the lakes and rivers of the world. Tales of creatures such as the Loch Ness Monster fascinate old and young alike, and continue to evoke curiosity and controversy in the scientific world.

Gazing across a glassy Scottish Loch framed by rugged, stunning scenery, it is impossible to believe that such a tranquil scene could be shattered by the antics of a massive, possibly prehistoric, monster lurking in the depths of the lake. Yet this is precisely what has happened on numerous occasions, if hundreds of people who claim to have seen a serpent-style creature are to be believed.

ACCOUNTS OF MORAG

'I looked up and saw about 20 yards [18m] behind us this creature coming directly after us in our wake. It only took a matter of seconds to catch up with us. It grazed the side of the boat, I am quite certain this was unintentional. When it struck, the boat seemed to come to a halt or at least slow down. I grabbed the oar and was attempting to fend it off, my one fear being that if it got under the boat it might capsize it.

Duncan McDonnell

'We watched it catch us up then bump into the side of the boat, the impact sent a kettle of water I was heating onto the floor. I ran into the cabin to turn the gas off as the water had put the flame out. Then I came out of the cabin to see my mate trying to fend the beast off with an oar, to me he was wasting his time. Then when I seen the oar break I grabbed my rifle and quickly putting a bullet in it fired in the direction of the beast.'

William Simpson

Loch Morar is believed to be home to the monster known as 'Morag'.

MORAG

One venue for several famous sightings has been Loch Morar, where the monster is known as 'Morag'. Fishermen Duncan McDonnell and William Simpson were afloat on 16 August 1969, when they had a close-quarters experience with this being of gigantic proportions.

It was 9pm and the fishermen's boat was travelling at a speed of about seven knots when a splash in the loch nearby caught the men's attention. Natural curiosity soon turned to terror as the thing churning the water made a bee-line straight for them. The shot was enough to see off the marauder, although neither of the men believed the bullet had wounded it. They estimated that the creature measured about 9m (30ft) in length and had a snake-like head extending some 0.5m (20in) above the water. Its skin was rough and brown. With a depth of 305m (1,000ft), Loch Morar is deeper than Loch Ness and its waters run clearer. If this were the home of a beast it would remain a private one, as there are no roads running around the loch. One rumour is that Morag is the ghost of a long-extinct dinosaur.

NESSIE

Meanwhile, in Loch Ness, a creature has been oft seen and sometimes even photographed. The first recorded witness to Nessie's exploits was St Columba, who allegedly saved a man from its attack. Sightings have escalated since 1933, when John McKay reported seeing 'an enormous animal rolling and plunging on the surface'. There have been photographs in abundance, most famously one taken in 1934, which made international headlines. However, most of the photos, including that one, have since been branded as fakes. Other sightings are usually assumed to be uprooted trees drifting in the wind.

In 2003 a BBC 'Nessie hunt' decided to test the waters using scientific expertise. The team sent 600 sonar beams into the loch without finding evidence of a deep-water creature. This result has fuelled the sceptics' cause, which assumes that Nessie has more to do with a buoyant tourist trade than any underwater phenomenon. There is insufficient food in the loch to support an animal of Nessie's dimensions and the sceptics claim that the

If the Loch Ness monster does exist, then perhaps it is rearing young in the depths of the loch, so the legend will continue into the future...

sightings are more likely to be of giant eels, catfish or sturgeons. However, they do not explain how the loch would provide enough food for these fish. (One sturgeon was found to be 3.75m (12ft) long, weighed 400kg (882lb) and achieved an age of 80 years.)

The latest attempt to debunk the Nessie story insists that the creatures spotted by witnesses were in fact elephants. During the 1930s, a travelling circus owned by Bertram Mills frequently fetched up on the banks of the loch and its elephants took a dip. The saga was stepped up by the sharp-witted impressario Mills, who offered a vast reward for capture of the Loch Ness monster, having realized his elephants were the root cause of a rash of sightings.

Yet still there are regular reports that Nessie has surfaced from people who are neither tourist trade operators nor circus proprietors, who appear to have no vested interest in proving her existence.

CHESSIE

Similar to 'Nessie' is 'Chessie', a long, dark, snake-like creature, which has been sighted on numerous occasions since the 19th century in the lake at Chesapeake Bay in the USA. Evidence of its existence has been captured on film by tourists, who continue to flock to the region in the hope of catching a glimpse of the mysterious serpent.

Further reports of Chessie emanate from respected members of the community, with witnesses including an

A photograph of 'Champ' in the waters of Lake Champlain in the northeast of the United States of America.

FBI agent, ex-CIA officials and coast guards. Although a fairly accurate description of the animal has been achieved – around 10m (33ft) long, about one third of a metre (1ft) in diameter and with a humped brown back – no one has yet been able to establish exactly what kind of serpent it is. Some have suggested that it may even be an example of a dinosaur that has somehow survived to this day.

CHAMP

Another snake is rumoured to inhabit the waters of Lake Champlain, on the borders of New York and Vermont. Affectionately nicknamed 'Champ', the animal is said to have been seen in the region ever since 1609. Efforts have been made to try to establish the exact location of this first sighting, thought to be off the St Lawrence estuary. The serpent then appears to have migrated to Port Henry, where it was spotted first by settlers in 1819 and then by the sheriff of Clinton County in 1883.

With regular sightings now made in Lake Champlain, there is huge curiosity about this animal and many visit the area to try to see the creature for themselves. One such individual was Sandra Mansi, who was lucky enough to capture the animal on film. Experts have since analysed her photograph and denied that any kind of deception or forgery has taken place. Since then, there have also been unconfirmed sightings of a second, smaller, beast swimming alongside the larger animal. Could this be evidence that a mating pair are alive and well in the region?

Certainly, many people have no doubt of the existence of creatures such as Champ, but a number of questions

An illustration of the Cryptoclidus dinosaur. Some have speculated that the lake monsters may be surviving dinosaurs.

A statue of the Ogopogo lake monster in Kelowna, British Columbia.

still remain unanswered. Are these animals examples of the pleiosaur, a species of dinosaur long since believed to be extinct? If so, how many are there? How long do they live for? And, if they are indeed modern-day dinosaurs, how did they manage to survive when all the others perished?

LAW OF THE DEEP

Meanwhile Canada, with its expansive wild terrain and deep lakes. has at least a trio of monsters to its name.

In Lake Pohenegamook, Quebec, the reported resident is Ponik, a 12m-long (39ft) beast with a horse's head, humps and two flippers. Over in British Columbia, in lake Okanagan, a creature called Ogopogo has been sighted on several occasions since 1850. The notion that something lives in the lake is so much ingrained into Canadian culture that, should the monster surface, it would be against British Columbian law to harm it. In Newfoundland, the Crescent Lake is reputedly the home of Cressie, a snake-like creature with a fishy head. Alleged appearances by all three in recent times have made headlines around the world.

The hunt continues for Selma, resident in Lake Seljordsvatnet in Norway. Also reportedly possessing a horse's head, Selma is said to be black, have flippers and measure somewhere between 3-12m (10–39ft) in length. Locals have reported sightings of their elusive neighbour since 1750.

The coelacanth fish was thought to have become extinct at around the same time as the dinosaurs, until it was discovered alive and well in 1938.

NOT SO EXTINCT

Perhaps, in light of these numerous reports, the time has come for a reassessment of traditional theories concerning the extinction of the pleiosaur. With little information available on both the prehistoric and supposed modern-day version of this dinosaur, however, and the fact that sightings are fairly rare, scientists are faced with a daunting task. Unless a breakthrough discovery is made, it seems likely that the truth surrounding these dark creatures of the deep will continue to elude humankind.

So can these really be supernatural beings or creatures isolated from a bygone age? The jury is still out on the exact identification of the creatures that reside in the lochs and lakes. Yet we do know that some things have survived in the deep for centuries, unknown to mankind. The most prominent example is the coelacanth, the so-called 'fossil fish' thought to pre-date the dinosaurs by millions of years, that was assumed to have become extinct at around the same time. Then, in 1938, it was discovered alive and well and living in South African waters. Because of the extreme sensitivity of its eyes, the coelacanth is rarely caught by fishermen during the daytime or on nights with a full moon. If the coelacanth remained hidden from man for many millions of years, then it is more than likely that other species elude us too.

Indeed, for all our technological advances, there are plenty of things about life in the murky depths of the world's vast inland waters that remain a mystery. It is tempting to believe that the Morag, Nessie and the rest of the world's lake monsters are among them.

BUNYIP

According to the Aboriginal dream of creation, deep in the heart of the Australian outback there lurks a mysterious creature known as the Bunyip. This beast is said to inhabit and defend lakes, swamps and billabongs, leaving its territory at night to venture into human dwellings to prey upon vulnerable women and children. Stories abound of its spine-chilling bellowing as it moves in search of its prey in and around the Australian waterways. But is this creature purely a fictional, symbolic warning about the very real dangers presented by the alligators that lurk in the inland waters of this vast continent? Or is there some truth behind the tales?

Among the Aborigines, there are varied descriptions of the Bunyip. Some say it is covered in feathers, others that it has scales like an alligator. Almost all describe the animal as having an equine tail, flippers and walrus-like tusks. These reports run counter, however, to the stories of the Bunyip related by the first Western settlers. Far from being a savage creature, these people describe the Bunyip as a kind of aquatic herbivore that lived in the waterways and peacefully grazed on the abundant grasses of the riverbanks and marshland.

These reports suggest that there were, in fact, two main species of Bunyip. The most often sighted of the two was the Dog-faced Bunyip, which, as its name suggests, possessed a canine face, a long, shaggy coat and small, wing-like flippers. The second species, the Long-necked Bunyip, apparently possessed a similar coat to the Dog-faced Bunyip, but with a longer neck, a horse-like mane, tusks and flippers.

There are numerous written and spoken accounts of encounters with Dog-faced Bunyips during the 19th and early-20th centuries. The creature was sighted in lakes, rivers and billabongs all over Australia and Tasmania. By contrast, reports of the rarer Long-necked Bunyip seem to be restricted to the state of New South Wales.

The sheer number and collaboratory nature of the stories seems to negate the possibility that these strange hybrid creatures belong purely to the realms of fantasy. But if they do exist in reality, what type of animal are they and where did they come from? And, most importantly from a conservational and cryptozoolological perspective, what has become of them?

Of the various theories in existence about the creature's origins, one in particular seems to have excited researchers, although many remain sceptical. The Bunyip bears a strong resemblance, both in its appearance and behaviour, to a supposedly extinct creature known as the Diprotodon, a large rhinoceros-sized herbivorous marsupial that roamed the land more than 10,000 years ago. Some experts believe that the Diprotodon was, like the Bunyip, equally at home on the land and in the water. Perhaps, then, in a land rich in marsupial diversity, the Diprotodon evolved over the course of thousands of years into a sort of marsupial hippo – the Bunyip? Although there are those who maintain that this might be possible, in general scientists have dismissed the notion that a few of these ancient animals may have somehow survived until the 20th century.

Another theory is that the Bunyip was, in fact, a seal and that the mystery is a simple case of repeated misidentification by inland locals who have never seen sea-dwelling seals. Similarly, it has been suggested that Bunyips might have been seals that migrated inland along the waterways, evolving to fit into their new surroundings by shedding their blubber and replacing it with thick fur.

These possibilities are also a matter of fierce debate, however. If the Bunyips were no more than seals, how could they have been observed grazing on land? Seals are aquatic mammals that feed on fish, not herbivorous grazers that are capable of living on land as well as in water. Moreover, the physical attributes of the Long-necked Bunyip do not match those of a seal.

There are many unanswered questions on the subject of the Bunyip, but it seems the truth will never be known. The Bunyip has not been seen for almost a century so if it really did exist, it may have perished as a result of environmental changes in the waterways and the effects of pollution. The only place in which it would seem to live on is in the imaginations and traditions of the local people in the areas in which this enigmatic creature was seen.

Aboriginal Australians tell of a dangerous beast lurking in the outback known as the Bunyip.

NANDI BEARS

Of all Africa's unexplained animals, the Nandi bear is said to be the most ferocious and is consequently the most feared. It is renowned all over this huge continent, where it strikes terror into the hearts of both native people and Westerners alike. The nature of its existence is a mystery – is it really a bear, or could it be some other kind of animal? And how has it managed to avoid categorization by scientists?

There would certainly appear to be a strange, unidentified killer animal prowling around the villages on the east coast of Africa. Numerous eyewitness reports describe the beast as resembling a large hyena, being about the same size as a lion and having a dark, possibly reddish-brown, coat. It is said to be a nocturnal creature, and there are numerous reports of vicious attacks on humans. It also has the thick, dark fur and shuffling gait commonly associated with members of the bear family.

Although it is known, from the writings of Pliny and others, that bears did once roam this continent, according to official animal demographic statistics, there are no native, wild bears living in Africa today. One type of bear did once roam the continent, but this species is thought to have become extinct during the Paleolithic period. With so many factors – such as the animal's shape, behaviour, appearance and ability to stand on its hind legs – suggesting that this creature might be a type of bear, it has been asked whether some of this supposedly extinct species could have managed to survive, and evade detection by scientists.

Although this so-called Atlas bear matches the descriptions of the modern-day Nandi bear, the identification raises a number of significant problems.

Not least of these issues is the fact that fossil

The Nandi bear is a ferocious killer that roams parts of East Africa, but what type of animal is it really?

A 1960s fanciful illustration of an encounter with a Nandi bear.

records of the Atlas bear have been found solely in northern Africa, whereas the Nandi bear is only located in the east of the country, yet not one single fossil record of the Nandi has been discovered on this continent.

Perhaps, then, this mysterious beast is not a bear at all? Many people believe instead that it is some sort of huge, bloodthirsty hyena, which could either be a previously undiscovered species, or else a remnant from prehistoric times. In support of this argument is the fact that archeologists have found evidence of the existence on the continent of a short-faced hyena, similar in size to a lion which lived until the Paleolithic era.

Others suggest that the creature could be a Chalicothere, a sloped-back animal related to the horse, but having claws instead of hooves. Like the hyena, this species is also believed to have become extinct in the Paleolithic era. Although this description matches that of the Nandi bear, there is one crucial factor which makes the proposition less likely: the Chalicothere, in common with all horses, was a herbivore, whereas the Nandi bear is known to be a vicious killer.

The Nandi tribe, from which the beast derives its name, describes the bear as a primate, resembling a large baboon. Baboons are omnivores, known to make savage attacks on animals such as smaller monkeys and sheep, and are also able to stand on two feet. Differences in behaviour between the baboon and the mysterious animal – such as the fact that the baboon hunts in packs and is not nocturnal – have been noted, but can possibly be ascribed to the fact that the two creatures could have a slightly different genetic make-up.

On the evidence provided by the fossils of giant baboons and the description of the Nandi tribe, researchers are seriously considering the possibility that the Nandi bear could be some sort of hitherto unknown species of baboon. Alternatively, it might be a survivor from prehistoric times.

Until more thorough research is carried out, however, or a specimen has been caught, scientists and cryptozoologists are unable to verify exactly what kind of animal this is. Only once this is known can they start to solve the riddle of its origination.

Some believe that the Nandi bear could be a type of especially bloodthirsty hyena.

An artist's impression of the Orang-Pendek. These legendary creatures are said to inhabit parts of Sumatra and Flores in Indonesia.

ORANG-PENDEK

Tales of mysterious ape-like creatures are not uncommon. Indeed, the possible existence of animals such as the Yeti or Bigfoot has gripped the imagination of mankind for many years, and is an endless source of debate and intrigue. One creature that has been the subject of marked interest in recent years is the Orang-Pendek or 'little man'.

Accounts of this animal come from a range of sources, most notably from the local people of Sumatra, who have accepted it as a part of the diverse habitat in which they live. It is, they say, a shy creature that only kills small animals for food and has never attacked a human. It is therefore not regarded as a threat and is generally left alone by the natives.

The Orang-Pendek is described as short in stature, walking on its hind legs at a height of just 0.7m–1.5m (2ft 3 in–4ft 11in). Its pinkish-brown skin is covered with a coat of short, dark body hair and it has long, flowing hair around its face. Its arms, unlike those of most normal apes, are considerably shorter than its legs, and it appears more human than ape-like.

Many footprints have been discovered over the years, and these have been used as proof of the animal's existence. Although these prints are said to resemble those made by a child of around seven years old, they are in fact much broader than a human's and some accounts actually describe the feet as pointing backwards.

To add to the natives' accounts of the Orang-Pendek, a number of sightings of the creature by Western explorers have further corroborated the story. The first sighting of the Orang-Pendek by a Westerner occurred in 1910. The man described it as: 'a large creature, low on its feet, which ran like a man and was about to cross my path; it was very hairy and it was not an orangutan; but its face was not like an ordinary man's'. This description was echoed by that of a Dutch hunter 13 years later, who added that he felt unable to kill the beast because its physical appearance was so similar to that of a human being.

More recently, in the late 1980s, interest in the animal was reignited by the findings of the English travel writer, Deborah Matyr. Although initially sceptical that such a creature did in fact exist, after sighting it on several occasions and studying its footprints, she went on to become one of its most reliable and trusted witnesses.

Following the emergence of poor-quality photographic evidence of the creature a decade later, it was decided that conclusive evidence of the Orang-Pendek was needed; as the shadowy and blurred images that had been captured on film were deemed to be inadequate proof of its existence. Accordingly, a number of expeditions have set out lately to the Sumatran swamps to try to gather definite proof. The discovery of hair and faecal samples, casts of footprints and a clear and incontrovertible photo, for example, would not only prove once and for all that this creature exists, but would enable scientists to determine if it is an example of a species of ape previously unknown to zoologists.

Scientists are, alternatively, debating whether the Orang-Pendek might be linked in some way to the discovery, in a limestone cave on the Indonesian island of Flores, of a new species of miniature human. Evidence has been uncovered to show that these tiny people, nicknamed 'hobbits' on account of their diminutive stature, lived and hunted on the island 18,000 years ago. Perhaps this creature is not an ape at all, but, rather, an example of a sub-species of human being? It seems that further evidence will be needed before a definitive answer to the mystery of the Orang-Pendek is provided.

KONGAMATO

Although dinosaurs are known to have been extinct for thousands of years, a strange tale emanating from African natives in Zambia might, in fact, suggest otherwise. Over the centuries there have been numerous reports of ferocious flying reptiles that bear an uncanny resemblance to a supposedly extinct species of dinosaur called the pterosaur.

These claims have inspired such curiosity that, in 1932, the traveller Frank H. Welland ventured into the Jiundu swamps in the Mwinilunga district of western Zambia to further investigate the story. The natives gave him detailed accounts of monstrous, reddish birds, with a wingspan of 1–2m (3–7ft), long beaks full of teeth and leathery skin in place of feathers. They called these creatures 'kongamato', which translates as 'overwhelmer of boats', due to the fact that the huge birds would often overturn small vessels, attacking and sometimes killing the occupants. So terrified were the locals of the kongamato that it was thought that just one look at it would result in certain death. Welland wrote an account of the natives' descriptions in his book, *In Witchbound Africa*, which received

An illustration of the kongamato, so-named for the terror they inflicted on boats.

great publicity for it also revealed that, when Welland showed the Zambians drawings of the prehistoric pterosaur, they unanimously and unhesitatingly agreed that these sketches identified precisely the creature they knew as the kongamato.

Many people were sceptical of these claims, and argued instead that the Zambian people had in fact obtained the description of the pterosaur from those natives who had worked on excavations in Tanzania where the fossilized bones of pterosaurs had been discovered some years earlier.

There are several problems with this theory, however. First, was it possible for descriptions of the dinosaur bones to have travelled from Tanzania to Zambia, a distance of 900km (559 miles)? Second, even if this had been the case, and the Zambians had heard about the skeletal structure of the pterosaur, how would they have known about the creature's leathery skin and lack of feathers? Finally, if the sightings were nothing more than the product of fervent imaginings, why was it that they did not come directly from the excavation site in Tanzania, rather than from as far away as Zambia?

Sightings of the mysterious creature continued, one story being told to the English newspaper correspondent, Mr G. Price, by a civil servant living in Africa. The expatriate recounted how he had met a native who had suffered an almost fatal wound to the chest while exploring the much-feared swampland. The man claimed that he had received his injury in an attack by a huge long-beaked bird.

Such stories were not limited to the inhabitants of the Zambian swamps, however. One account came from the famous zoologist and writer Ivan Sanderson who, in 1933, was leading an expedition to the Assumbo Mountains in Cameroon on behalf of the British Museum. He described how, while out hunting one day, he had shot a fruit bat over the fast-flowing river. Wading out into the water to retrieve the fallen animal, Sanderson lost his balance and fell. Having regained his footing, he heard a warning yell from one of his colleagues and to his horror saw a monstrous black creature bearing down upon him from the sky at great speed.

Sanderson ducked into the river to escape the huge bird and then made for the riverbank. At this point, the creature renewed its attack, diving down on him again and both he and his companion threw themselves on the ground, conscious only of the sound of the beating of the creature's powerful wings. Fortunately, the animal then flew off into the night, leaving the two men to return to the safety of their camp. Here, they related their story to the natives, asking them if they knew what their attacker might have been. The locals fled in terror without answering the question.

Sanderson reflected on what he had seen – fortunately, he had had sufficient time to note the physical appearance of the creature and, due to his zoological expertise, was able to give a precise description of the animal. He

Could the kongamato actually be the long-extinct pterosaur?

described it as having been about the size of an eagle, with a semicircle of sharp white teeth in its lower jaw. This report matched not only those of other sightings, but also corresponded with what is known of the pterosaur. Sanderson also remarked that the beast, like the pterosaur, resembled a bat. However, he discounted the possibility that it was only a fruit bat on the basis that these creatures are not known to attack humans.

Some years later, in 1942, similar stories from other areas in Africa, such as Mount Kilimanjaro and Mount Kenya, were related to the author, Captain C. Pitman. They described the existence of a large bat-like bird, which produced tracks suggesting that it had a large tail that dragged along the ground behind the creature.

In his book *A Game Warden Takes Stock*, Captain Pitman went on to describe how the animals were alleged to feed on rotting human flesh if corpses were not buried to a sufficient depth. Further accounts of the birds were contained in another publication, *Old Fourlegs*, in which fossil expert Dr J. L. B. Smith described 'flying dragons' in the region of Mount Kilimanjaro.

Today the sightings continue in remote areas of Africa. In 1998, a Kenyan exchange student, Steve Romando-Menya, declared that the existence of the kongamato is common knowledge among the bush dwellers in his country. Moreover, all witnesses, when asked to draw what they have seen, are repeatedly reported to draw a pterosaur.

What are these mysterious creatures? Sceptics claim that it is impossible for the prehistoric pterosaur to be in existence today, and yet the number of confirmed reports from reliable sources would seem to indicate otherwise. The controversy and debate continue to this day.

Reports of similar flying creatures were also heard from the region around Mount Kilimanjaro.

Ivan T. Sanderson, the zoologist and writer, had a similar experience in Cameroon, when a huge bird dived and attacked.

MOKELE-MBEMBE

For hundreds of years, natives living in the depths of the African jungle have spoken of a large, water-dwelling beast unfamiliar to Western science. It is known by a variety of names and has been sighted by many of the local population, but has yet to be positively identified or photographed by anybody from outside the area. So does it really exist and, if so, what type of creature is it?

Explorers travelling across the vast continent of Africa in the 1900s were told many tales about strange beasts, most of which are now as familiar to us as normal domestic pets. Among these stories were repeated claims by tribesmen that they shared their land with swamp-dwelling creatures the size of an elephant and possessing a long neck and tail. Evidence of the animals could be seen in their rounded tracks, containing three claw marks, on the banks of the local rivers.

In 1932, a cryptozoologist, Ivan Sanderson, discovered animal tracks resembling those of the hippopotamus in an area in which no such animals lived. On discussing his find with the native people, he was told that the animal responsible for making such unusual footprints was known as the mbulu-eM'bembe. Later that day, he caught sight of a creature, in the water, that appeared to be larger than a hippopotamus, but it disappeared under the surface before he had the chance to make a closer inspection.

The same animal is known to the pigmy tribes of the Likouala region of the Republic of Congo. They call the creature Mokele-mbembe, which means 'rainbow', 'one that stops the flow of rivers' or 'monstrous animal', depending on who is using the term. They describe the animals, which must seem particularly huge to them given their diminutive stature, as being hairless vegetarians, with reddish-brown or grey skin and a neck that is more than 3m (10ft) in length. Interestingly, their description of the animals' tracks is the same as that given by Ivan Sanderson.

Since 1932, many more scientists and explorers have visited these areas in the hope of catching a glimpse of the elusive monster. Unfortunately, none of them has ever witnessed anything, although, according to natives, a creature with a long neck and tail was killed near Lake Tele in 1959. If this mysterious creature does exist, what kind of animal is it? Eyewitness reports would seem to suggest that the animal strongly resembles a sauropod dinosaur. This theory was put to the test by James Powell, an American explorer, who visited the area with the aim of solving the mystery. On showing a picture of a sauropod to the many tribes who said they had seen the animal, all instantly confirmed that the Mokele-mbembe was indeed a sauropod.

Dinosaurs are believed to have become extinct many millions of years ago, so how could the sauropod have survived when the rest of these prehistoric creatures perished? One explanation for their continuing existence might be the fact that their remote habitat is more similar than anywhere else on the planet to the environment in which the original sauropod would have lived. It has also been suggested that they owe their survival to their innate shyness, which has kept them hidden from curious, prying and potentially harmful eyes.

Whatever the nature of these enigmatic beasts, they are undoubtedly central to the debate about cryptozoology. If indeed they do exist, and could be proved to do so, this would overturn centuries of thought about the natural history of our planet and our own evolution.

The Mokele-mbembe was said to strongly resemble sauropod dinosaurs like the Brontosaurus.

THE VENEZUELAN APEMAN

The notorious photograph taken by de Loys shows the dead ape sitting on a crate, propped up by a stick.

It is among the most notorious images in the annals of natural history. Seated on a gasoline crate, and propped up grotesquely by a stick, the dead ape had been photographed in a mountainous forest district of Venezuela. The problem for early 20th-century zoologists was that no such animal was believed to exist in the continent of the Americas.

The photograph was taken around 1920 by François de Loys, a Swiss geologist on a three-year expedition to explore rivers and swamps southwest of Lake Maracaibo. Their aim was to identify lucrative oil reserves, but it was a mission that extracted a heavy price from de Loys and his men. Of the original 20-strong party only four survived; the others were all victims of disease or attacks by hostile local tribes.

During the last year of the survey, the beleaguered group was camped beside the Tarra River when two red-haired creatures around 1.5m (5ft) tall emerged from the forest in an excitable state. De Loys thought at first they were bears, but as they moved closer he realized they were apes, probably male and female. The animals screamed, waved their arms, broke off branches (seemingly to use as weapons), defecated into their hands and threw their faeces at the camp.

This type of behaviour is a common aggressive response among spider monkeys and some apes and it suggested an attack was imminent. De Loys did what any self-respecting European explorer would do under the circumstances and shot them, to defend himself and his party. The female was killed and the injured male ran off into the jungle.

Gathering around the carcass, everyone in the party agreed that the species was extremely unusual. Native guides said they had never seen anything quite like it and de Loys, although not a zoologist, realized it might be of interest. Unfortunately, given the circumstances, the chances of getting the body back to Europe in a recognizable state were non-existent. De Loys decided to take a photograph as documentary evidence, and the picture was taken from a distance of about 3m (10ft) away.

What happened next is not clear. Some reports suggest the flesh was cooked and eaten by de Loys' men; others that the remains were partly preserved and later lost in a battle with Motilones Indians. Either way, when de Loys finally returned home, his only evidence was the photo.

Curiously, it was nine years before this emerged. Even then, it was not de Loys who presented it to the scientific establishment but one of his close friends, George Montandon, a Swiss anthropologist, who apparently chanced on the picture while inspecting some of de Loys' ageing files. Montandon published it in the *Illustrated London News*, naming the creature *Ameranthropides Loysi*, in honour of its intrepid discoverer.

Soon after this, the Academy of Science in Paris met to discuss the implications of the find. The cornerstone of primate evolution theory was that apes and humans emerged only in the Old World, and specifically Africa. If, after all, they were present in the Americas, then long-established rules would have to be rewritten. It would be a leap in the dark and, unsurprisingly, the Academy did not take it. The scientists concluded that the animal was a sapajou, a fairly common New World monkey. The only evidence to the contrary, they argued, was its size and lack of a tail. Assessment of size was dependent on de Loys' word and the tail could have been either cut off or tucked out of shot. The ape theory was further undermined when sceptics waded into the debate.

Sir Arthur Keith implied that the animal was a spider monkey, while others went further, accusing de Loys of blatantly fabricating a crude hoax. Throughout the 20th century the same questions were asked: Why did de Loys not photograph a man beside the ape to provide size context? Why such an odd pose? Why wait nine years before allowing a friend to reveal such a major discovery? And so on.

As late as 1996, cryptozoologist Loren Coleman, writing in the *Anomalist Magazine*, argued that George Montandon had been working to a secret racist agenda. This theory held that different races were descended from different apes and consequently some were superior to others. Until the Venezuelan apeman appeared, Montandon had struggled to explain which ape was the ancestor of native American Indians.

In fact, the hoax argument is itself hardly watertight. For one thing why would de Loys, a serious geologist, wish to risk the wrath of the scientific establishment by pulling a silly stunt in an area outside his expertise? Secondly, in an expedition dogged by disease and violent deaths, he surely had more urgent priorities – such as getting home alive. And as for the nine-year delay, isn't it possible that de Loys did not appreciate the significance of what he had seen? Supporters point

out that an analysis of the gasoline crate seat revealed it was 50cm (20in) high, putting the de Loys creature at 1.55m (4ft 11in), almost exactly the height he claimed in his report. If so this would certainly rule out a spider monkey, which has an average height of between 38–68cm (15–27in). Other researchers say that while there are some likenesses to a spider monkey – the round ridges surrounding the eyes, the long hair and long fingers and toes – there are also several contradictory features. These include the shape of the face (oval rather than triangular) the lack of a prognathism (a protruding lower jaw) and a highly prominent forehead.

If Montandon had been alone in reporting a mysterious ape-like animal in the Americas, his claim would be easier to dismiss. But in fact there are many accounts. A chronicle written in 1533 by the conquistador Pedro de Cieza refers to a Spaniard finding one dead in the woods. In the 18th-century Edward Bancroft, doctor, naturalist and British spy, recounted Indian legends of a 1.5m-tall (4ft 11in) creature which walked upright and was covered in hair. Nineteenth century science writer Philip Gosse, in his *Essay on the Natural History of Guyana*, suggests the existence of 'a large anthropoid ape not yet recognized by zoologists', and in 1876 explorer Charles Barrington Brown wrote of a beast dubbed 'Didi' by Guyanese Indians – 'a powerful wild man whose body is covered in hair and who lives in the forest.' More recently, in 1987, an American mycologist called Gary Samuels was working in Guyana, courtesy of a grant from the New York Botanical Gardens. Hearing footsteps, he looked up from his inspection of fungi to see a 1.5m-tall (4ft 11in), bipedal, ape-like animal which bellowed at him before running away.

It is easy to dismiss the de Loys photograph as a hoax, perhaps because we are uncomfortable with the idea that such a significant species could exist without our knowledge. Yet natural history is littered with similar examples – the okapi, the Komodo dragon and the coelacanth were all 20th-century finds – and there remain surprisingly large swathes of the planet that have not been properly explored. De Loys may be a charlatan... but the jury is still out.

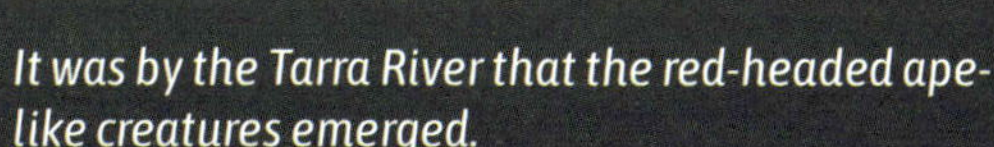

It was by the Tarra River that the red-headed ape-like creatures emerged.

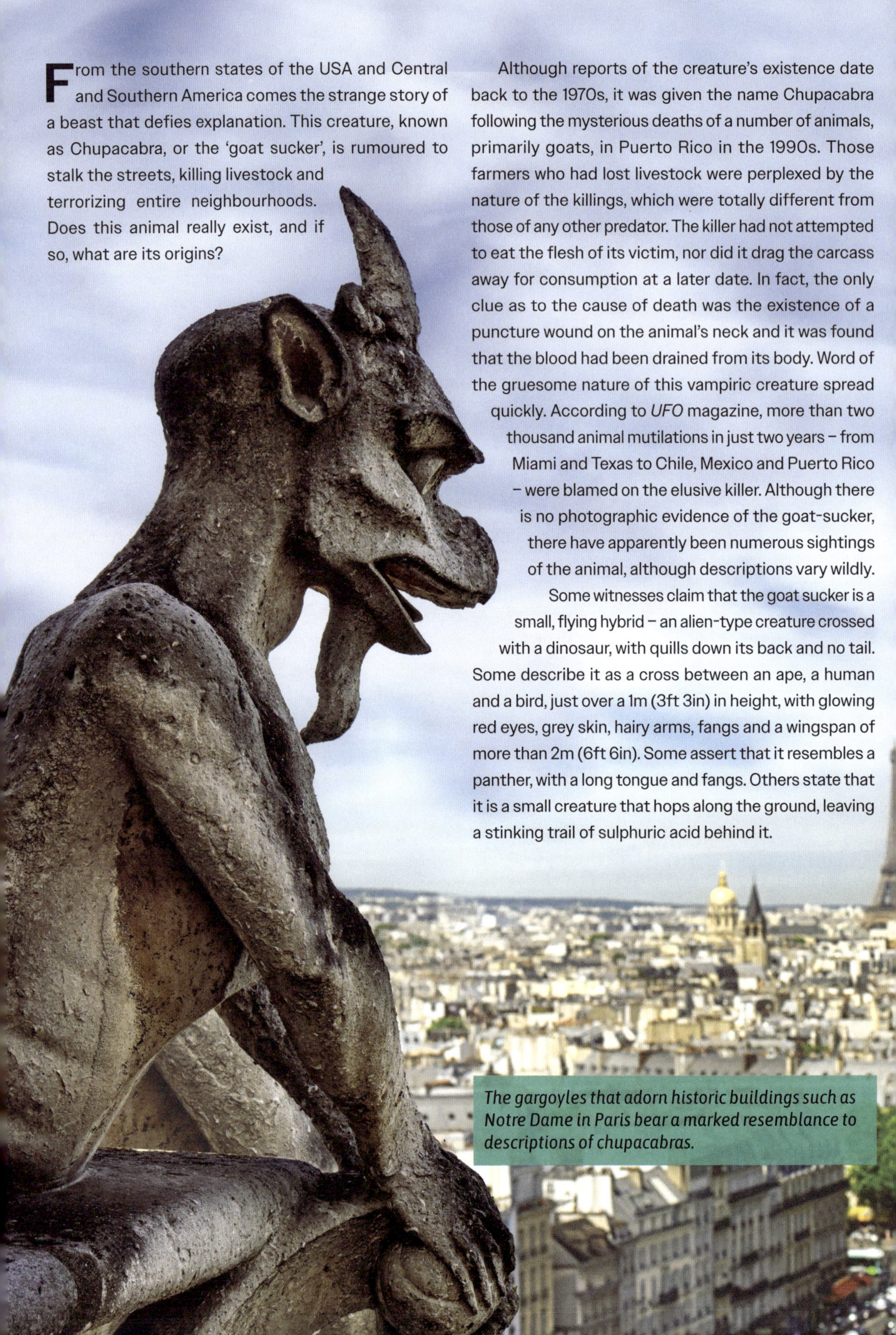

From the southern states of the USA and Central and Southern America comes the strange story of a beast that defies explanation. This creature, known as Chupacabra, or the 'goat sucker', is rumoured to stalk the streets, killing livestock and terrorizing entire neighbourhoods. Does this animal really exist, and if so, what are its origins?

Although reports of the creature's existence date back to the 1970s, it was given the name Chupacabra following the mysterious deaths of a number of animals, primarily goats, in Puerto Rico in the 1990s. Those farmers who had lost livestock were perplexed by the nature of the killings, which were totally different from those of any other predator. The killer had not attempted to eat the flesh of its victim, nor did it drag the carcass away for consumption at a later date. In fact, the only clue as to the cause of death was the existence of a puncture wound on the animal's neck and it was found that the blood had been drained from its body. Word of the gruesome nature of this vampiric creature spread quickly. According to *UFO* magazine, more than two thousand animal mutilations in just two years – from Miami and Texas to Chile, Mexico and Puerto Rico – were blamed on the elusive killer. Although there is no photographic evidence of the goat-sucker, there have apparently been numerous sightings of the animal, although descriptions vary wildly.

Some witnesses claim that the goat sucker is a small, flying hybrid – an alien-type creature crossed with a dinosaur, with quills down its back and no tail. Some describe it as a cross between an ape, a human and a bird, just over a 1m (3ft 3in) in height, with glowing red eyes, grey skin, hairy arms, fangs and a wingspan of more than 2m (6ft 6in). Some assert that it resembles a panther, with a long tongue and fangs. Others state that it is a small creature that hops along the ground, leaving a stinking trail of sulphuric acid behind it.

The gargoyles that adorn historic buildings such as Notre Dame in Paris bear a marked resemblance to descriptions of chupacabras.

CHUPACABRA

The debate concerning the creature's appearance is only one of a number of questions to surround the Chupacabra. Of more importance to many is the conundrum of its origins – just where does it come from, and why is it here?

Of the many theories that abound, three have a particularly strong following. Some believe that the beast might be a species of dinosaur, previously unknown to man, that has managed to survive to this day. Some think that it is a type of extra-terrestrial pet, abandoned by aliens during an expedition to this planet. There are others who assume that this 'Anomalous Biological Entity' (as creatures such as the Chupacabra are known by UFO enthusiasts) is the consequence of a disastrous genetic experiment that endeavoured to combine the genes of an alien with those of an earthly animal.

Whether such an experiment was performed by humans or aliens is a matter of much controversy, which has been further fuelled by the results of blood analysis from a creature believed to be a dead Chupacabra. This report states that the animal's blood is unlike that of any known earthly animal. Whether this is due to the advanced scientific nature of any genetic manipulation that might have taken place or to the fact that the animal is an extra-terrestrial being is not clear.

The identity of this curious beast remains shrouded in mystery. Whether it is an unknown species of dinosaur, a creature of alien origin or indeed a specimen of advanced genetic engineering is a matter that may never be fully resolved, although no doubt the speculation will continue until a definitive answer is found.

Could the attacks on farm animals have been carried out by starving vampire bats, desperate for food?

THE JERSEY DEVIL

The malevolent figure of the devil is a symbol of evil that is present in almost every society and religion in the world. Throughout the ages, mankind has sought an answer to the question of its existence – is it a purely mythical creature, or could it be grounded in reality? Sightings of a terrifying otherworldly creature in New Jersey may clarify some of this uncertainty.

Numerous stories exist about the origins of the beast, although none of these versions has been conclusively proven. The tales contain slight variations in terms of the date, location, parentage and physical

The house in Leeds Point where Jane Leeds (neé Shroud) supposedly gave birth to the Jersey Devil.

Stephen Decatur supposedly fired a cannonball at the creature, but it mysteriously appeared unscathed by the encounter.

appearance of the demon, but there are, interestingly, some common themes running through the tales. The most obvious of these is the occurrence of the word 'Leeds' in separate accounts.

One of the most popular legends attributes the birth of the demon to a Mrs Shrouds of Leeds Point, who apparently made an ominous vow that if she ever became pregnant again, she desired the child to be a devil. Imagine her horror when she conceived shortly afterwards. When the boy was born, he was afflicted with terrible deformities, so she kept the child at home, away from prying eyes. The story relates how, one day, the infant started to flap his arms, which suddenly transformed themselves into a bat's wings. He then flew out of the open window into the night, never to be seen again.

Another account tells of a young girl living in Leeds Point who fell in love with an English soldier and became pregnant. Soon after this, he broke her heart by leaving the area with his division. The girl was shunned and cursed by the community, and nine months later gave birth to the devil.

While opinion is divided about the details of the conception and birth of the devil, there are no arguments about the sightings. The strange being is said to have been seen by more than 2,000 people over the last 260 years, causing havoc in the small towns surrounding the New Jersey Pine Barrens. Factories

Is this the image of the devilish creature that has haunted New Jersey for centuries?

and schools have closed down as a result and whole communities have been consumed by fear. Sightings of the creature have taken place primarily in three distinct time periods – prior to 1909, during the week of 16–23 January 1909, and after 1909 – and they are corroborated by written eyewitness accounts.

Prior to 1909, encounters with the supernatural beast were frequent. Among those who saw the devil were Joseph Bonaparte (brother of Napoleon and former king of Spain) and the naval figure, Commodore Stephen Decatur, who actually shot the flying creature with a cannon ball. Amazingly, however, this action caused it no visible harm.

From 1840-41 there were numerous reports of farm animals being killed by an unknown creature that had an eerie, alien scream and left strange tracks behind it.

As the century progressed, these reports became more frequent, and many domestic animals were seen being carried off by a mysterious predator. On a visit to the region, the Mayor of New York noted that the local residents seemed terrified, and refused to leave their homes after dark.

Then, in one highly dramatic week, there was the most concentrated number of sightings to date. From 16–23 January 1909, the devil was seen by more than 1,000 people and its tracks were evident all over South Jersey and Philadelphia. Although there was a slight variation in the descriptions given of the creature that week, all said that it was able to fly, that it had a spine-chilling, otherworldly scream, and left strange prints in the snow. Trappers were mystified by the prints, which they had apparently never seen before, and were astonished to see that the trail went over rooftops and up trees. Attempts at hunting the animal were further thwarted by the fact that the tracker dogs refused to go near the prints.

During that week, the most prolonged close sighting of the beast occurred in Gloucester, outside the house belonging to Mr and Mrs Evans. The couple observed the creature for ten minutes, and reported that it had a head like a collie dog, but the face of a horse. It was about 1m (3ft 3in) in height, with a long neck and a large wingspan. It walked on its hind legs, which were similar to those of a crane, but had hooves instead of claws. The strange hybrid quality of this animal bears similarities to other reports, which describe it as a strange bird with glowing eyes and a horse's head.

Sightings of the animal both in the air and on the ground continued throughout the week, striking fear into the heart of the community and evoking intense speculation. Many attempts were made to capture or kill the creature, but it managed to escape every time.

Since 1909, the sightings have continued, although to a lesser extent. This decline could be attributed to a more cynical society, in which people are reluctant to make known their stories for fear of ridicule.

A number of theories have been put forward to explain the creature. Some believe that it is a scrowfoot duck, although this does not accord with the size of the animal as reported by witnesses. Others think it is a sand crane, which has not been seen in the region for many years. While similarities exist between the size and some of the behavioural patterns of this animal and accounts of the demonic creature, there is still no explanation for the horse's head, bat's wings, hooves or glowing eyes, or, for that matter, for the attacks on domestic animals.

A scientific theory that has been put forward is that the devil may be a relic from the Jurassic period, such as a pterodactyl, that has somehow managed to survive since that period, hiding away underground or in a cave. While this is perhaps possible, the description of the creature does not match that of any dinosaur from this era in history.

More superstitious explanations are based on the notion that the creature is the embodiment of evil and a harbinger of bad tidings or impending conflict. The dates of some of the sightings appear to support this idea, with reports being recorded shortly before the Civil War, the Spanish American War, World War I, World War II and the Vietnam War.

Whatever the origin and purpose of this intriguing being, it seems that its existence is beyond question. The frequency, reliability and time span of the sightings rule out the possibility that it is merely a creature of myth, or that events surrounding its appearance are all an elaborate hoax. Moreover, it looks likely that the creature is here to stay.

Speculation continues in New Jersey about the possible circumstances of the next sighting.

Some have suggested that reports of the Jersey Devil have been mistaken sightings of sand cranes – though there are many elements that do not add up with that explanation.

SKINWALKERS

The state of Utah is home to numerous supernatural occurrences and strange beings. Of these, the so-called 'skinwalker', or 'Wendigo', is perhaps the most terrifying and the question of its existence continues to mystify and bewilder the inhabitants of this part of the USA.

According to native Indian legend, the skinwalkers are a band of shape-shifting Navajo witches that roam the countryside terrorizing humans and animals alike. They can take on the form of any animal at any given moment, acquiring the inherent strengths and attributes of that particular creature while at the same time retaining their innate human cunning.

This ability to maintain human intelligence while gaining the sensory or speed advantages of a specific animal renders the skinwalker a truly awe-inspiring and formidable foe. In addition to the possession of everyday human knowledge, these witches are blessed with those powers that lie outside the realms of common wisdom. So a witch in the guise of a coyote will have amazing agility, strength and speed, combined with the dark powers of mind control and a knowledge of curses and other occult crafts. Native tradition relates that the skinwalkers have no choice about their metamorphoses, and that each change causes them much pain and torment. Perhaps it is for this reason that they show such ferocity towards the creatures around them, jealous of their ability to maintain a fixed identity and so remain exempt from the perpetual torment of mutability.

As a result of the witches' constantly changing identity, very little is known about their origins or habits. Many believe that they are linked to a region called 'Skinwalker Ridge' which, according to extra-terrestrial enthusiasts, is close to a region of intense UFO activity and which native Indians studiously avoid. Could this region be a portal to another dimension from which the shape-shifters originate? Some people think so.

What is known about these eerie beings has been gleaned from the many reports in existence. Sightings by Navajo Indians tell of the creature's glowing yellow eyes and ability to strike terror into even the bravest observer. Encounters are not restricted to the Navajos, however, as the events of 1983 show. The isolated

stretch of Route 163 that runs through the heart of the Monument Valley Navajo Tribal Park, although stunningly beautiful, is renowned for being the site of strange, otherworldly activities and local people warn outsiders that they should never venture into the region at night.

On this particular occasion, four members of a family were returning home from Wyoming, where they had been visiting friends. The most direct route was along Route 163, and having driven along this road without incident on the outward journey, they thought nothing of taking this course again on the way home.

The family reported that, on this pitch-black, moonless summer's evening, they had been driving for several hours without seeing another human being. They were making steady progress when the father who was driving, mentioned that they were no longer alone. Looking behind them, the whole family saw headlights some distance behind the car.

They continued on their journey, keeping the distant

Skinwalkers are witches with the ability to shapeshift into different creatures. They use their new and powerful forms to terrorize the local communities.

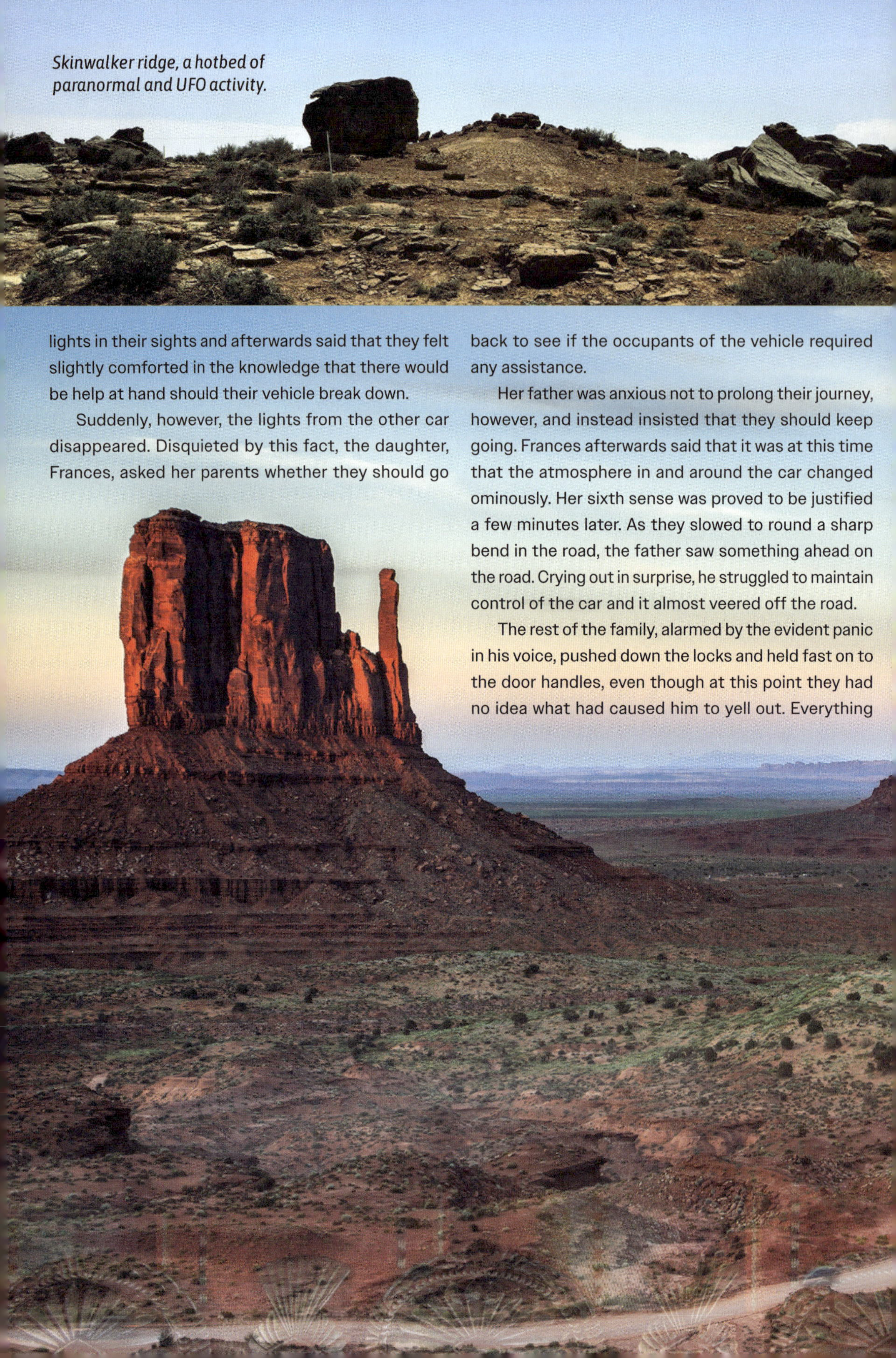

Skinwalker ridge, a hotbed of paranormal and UFO activity.

lights in their sights and afterwards said that they felt slightly comforted in the knowledge that there would be help at hand should their vehicle break down.

Suddenly, however, the lights from the other car disappeared. Disquieted by this fact, the daughter, Frances, asked her parents whether they should go back to see if the occupants of the vehicle required any assistance.

Her father was anxious not to prolong their journey, however, and instead insisted that they should keep going. Frances afterwards said that it was at this time that the atmosphere in and around the car changed ominously. Her sixth sense was proved to be justified a few minutes later. As they slowed to round a sharp bend in the road, the father saw something ahead on the road. Crying out in surprise, he struggled to maintain control of the car and it almost veered off the road.

The rest of the family, alarmed by the evident panic in his voice, pushed down the locks and held fast on to the door handles, even though at this point they had no idea what had caused him to yell out. Everything became all too clear when he slammed on the brakes to prevent the vehicle from careering over the edge of a steep drop.

Leaping towards their vehicle was a creature unlike any the family had ever seen before. Although dressed in a man's clothing, the monstrous being could not be described, by any stretch of the imagination, as a normal human.

Describing the course of events later to a Navajo friend, Frances recalled that the beast was black and very hairy, with long arms which clung on to the side of the car, and an anguished face that stared in at them for a few seconds before they sped away along the road.

Having reached the relative civilization of the nearest town, the family felt able to discuss the terrifying sight that they had recently witnessed. Shaken by what had happened, they were keen to see some evidence that their imagination had not been responsible for the strange events, and so made a thorough inspection of the car. Incredibly, there was not one single mark or print to be seen in the thick dust that had inevitably accumulated on the vehicle during its long journey. Neither was there any sign in the town of the vehicle that had been following them until the time of its sudden disappearance.

Although reports of encounters with the skinwalkers in one form or another are not uncommon among the Navajo, what is notable about this occurrence is that this family was not of native Indian origin.

Among the many questions to be raised by these bizarre happenings are the following: why were these people chosen by the strange supernatural beings? And what did they want from them?

These curious shape-shifting witches have aroused great debate in this part of the USA and all over the world. Other beings that are said to possess a similar mutability are the werewolves of European renown, which also have the same ability to inspire awe and terror in the unlucky observer.

The provenance and purpose of these malevolent beings remains a matter of intense controversy and, until more evidence comes to light, the mystery will continue.

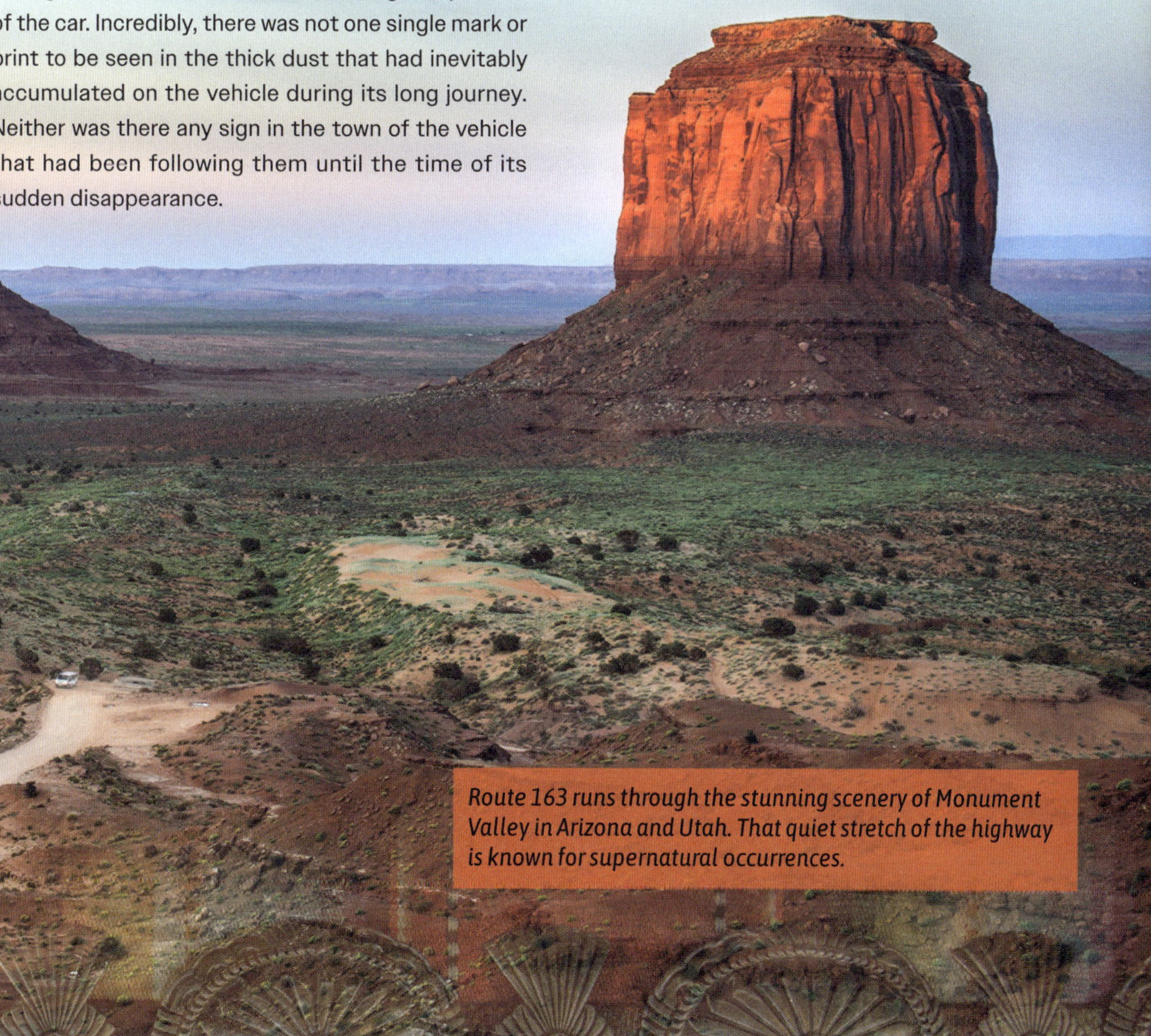

Route 163 runs through the stunning scenery of Monument Valley in Arizona and Utah. That quiet stretch of the highway is known for supernatural occurrences.

INDEX

Abdul Hamid III, Sultan 146
Adare, Lord 106
Amen-Ra 54, 55
Anasazi civilization 48–9
Antoinette, Marie 146
Aratake, Kihachiro 68, 70
Arigo, Jose 108–9
Arthur, King 76–9
Arthur Stone 76–9
Atlantis 64–7, 70, 93
Baalbeck 56–7
Barham, HMS 86–7
Barhuis, George 153
Barris, George 151–2, 153
Bender, Hans 136–7
Bey, Habib 146
Black Hope curse 158–61
Blavatsky, Helena 90–5
'Bloop' noise 168
Bonaparte, Joseph 200
Brahan Seer 124–7
Briggs, Benjamin Spooner 28
Briggs, Sarah 28
Briggs, Sohpia Matilda 28
Brown, Charles Barrington 195
Bunyip 180–1
Burr, F.L. 106
Carmichael, H. 84
Carnarvon, Lord 144, 145
Carter, Howard 144–5
Cartier, Pierre 147
Cayce, Edgar 67, 128–31
Chaco Canyon 48, 49
Champ 177–8
Chan Chan 50–1
Chariots of the Gods (von Daniken) 74
Charlton, Mr 84
Chessie 176–7
Christie, Agatha 12–13
Christie, Archie 12
Chupacabra 196–7
Ciudad Blanca 46–7
Colot, Jacques 146
Conan Doyle, Arthur 31, 84
Cooper, D.B. 20–3
Cornstalk, Chief 154–7
Cortes, Hernando 46
Coster, Ian D. 84
Cressie 179
Crookes, Sir William 107
Cyclops, USS 36–7
Darvill, Timothy 61–2
Davis, E. Wade 149
De Kersauson, Olivier 172
de Loys, François 192, 193–5
Dean, James 150–3
Decatur, Stephen 199, 200
Delphic oracle 116–17
Deminka, Natasha 110–13
Deveau, Oliver 28
Devine, Thomas E. 26–7
Dieterien, Germaine 42
Dixon, Jeane 100–1
Dogon tribe 42–5
Duncan, Helen 86–7
Earhart, Amelia 24–7
Earls of Mar 162–5
Edward VII, King 17
Elizabeth I, Queen 121
Eschrich, William F. 151
Eugenie, Empress 106
Evans, Mr and Mrs 200
Eyewitness: the Amelia Earhart Incident (Devine) 26–7
Fals, Heinrich 146
Fals, Wilhelm 146
Fay, Charles Edey 28, 31
Felix-Mentor, Felicia 148
Fesel, Heinrich 138
Flight 19 32–5
Fosdyk, Abel 30, 31
Fox, Christopher 169
Game Warden Takes Stock, A (Pitman) 188
Garden of Eden 65
Garrett, Eileen 82–5
Gehman, Ann 97
Geoffrey of Monmouth 77
Goebbels, Josef 138
Gosse, Philip 195
Griale, Marcel 42
Gruber, Elber 136–7
Haney, Sam and Judith 159–60, 161
Hawkins, Gerald 62, 74
Henry II, King 119
Hermania 31
Hess, Rudolf 138, 139
Hetepheres I, Queen 52
Hitchcock, Alfred 15
Hitler, Adolf 121, 136, 138–9
Home, Daniel Dunglas 104–7
Holy Grail 78
Hood, Lady 127
Hope, Francis 146
Hope diamond 146–7
Huaca de la Luna 50–1
Hurricane Andrew 141
Isis Unveiled (Blavatsky) 93
Jacobite Rebellion 164
Jersey Devil 198–201
Jupiter, USS 37
Kanilovsky, Prince 146

Kennedy, John F. 100–1
Khufu, King 52–3, 54
kongamato 186–9
Kosak, Paul 74
Krafft, Karl Ernest 138–9
Kraken 170–3
Kulagina, Ninel 102–3
Lammers, Arthur 129
Leeds, Jane 198, 199
Loch Ness monster 175–6
Lombroso, Cesare 88
Louis XIV, King 146
Lucan, Lord 10–11
Mackenzie, Kenneth 124, 127
Mansi, Sandra 177
Mary Celeste, The 28–31
Matyr, Deborah 185
McDonnell, Duncan 174, 175
McHenry, Carl 152
McKay, John 175
McLean, Evelyn Walsh 147
Medici, Catherine de 119
Miller, Glen 38–9
Mills, Bertram 176
Minoan civilization 65–6
Moche civilization 50–1
Mokele-mbembe 190–1
Montespan, Madame de 146
Montharides, Simon 146
Morag 174–5
Morehouse, David 28
Morris, Christopher 76
Mu 70, 71
Nandi bears
Napoleon III, Emperor 106
Narcisse, Clairvius 148–9
Nazca lines 72–5
Nennius 79
Nereus, USS 37
Newgrange tombs 58–9
Noonan, Fred 26–7
Norton, Jasper 159
Nostradamus 118–21
Nott, Julian 75
Ogopogo 179
Old Fourlegs (Smith) 188
Orang-Pendek 184–5
Palladino, Eusapia 88–9
Pitman, C. 188
Plato 64, 65, 66, 146
Pliny 182
Point Pleasant 156–7
Ponik 178–9
Price, G. 187
Price, Harry 83–4
Proteus, USS 37
pyramids of Giza 52–5, 59
R101 airship 84–5
Reagan, Ronald 98, 99
Reichardt, Frederick 17–18
Reiche, Maria 74
Renier, Noreen 96–9
Renner, Frumentius 136
Republic, The (Plato) 146
Rill, Andreas 134, 136–7
Rivett, Sandra 11
Roberston, Morgan 132
Roentgen, Wilhelm Conrad 110
Royal Norfolk Regiment 16–19
Samuels, Gary 195
Sanderson, Ivan 187–8, 189, 190
Sangoma, The 122–3
Scallion, Gordon 140–1
Schoch, Robert M. 70
Seaforth, Isabella 127
Secret Doctrine, The (Blavatsky) 93
Sextus V, Pope 119
Simpson, William 174, 175
skinwalkers 202–5
Skolnick, Andrew 112
'Slowdown' noise 168–9
Smith, J.B.L.
Society for Physical Research 89
Speculum Regale 171
Spielberg, Stephen 33
Stonehenge 59, 60–3
Story of the Mary Celeste, The (Fay) 31
Tavernier, Jean-Baptiste 146
Taylor, Charles 33, 34
Theosophical Movement 92–3
Theremin, Leon 14–15
Thom, Alexander 62
Thomas, Betty and Charlie 159
Titanic sinking 132–3
Traits of Astro-Biology (Krafft) 138
Tutankhamen, King 144–5
Venezuelan apeman 192–5
Villiers, Major 84
von Daniken, Erich 74–5
Wainwright, Geoffrey 61–2, 76, 79
Welland, Frank 186
Williams, Ben and Jean 160–1
Woodman, Jim 75
Wreck of the Titan, The (Roberston) 132
Yonaguni 68–71
Zachariah 78
zombies 148–9

PICTURE CREDITS

t = top, b = bottom, l = left, r = right

Alamy: 13, 30, 70, 82r, 83, 100, 105, 128, 150, 151, 152, 164, 175

Bridgeman Images: 12, 29

Corbis: 24, 144, 147, 200

David Woodroffe: 27, 31, 35, 71

FBI: 22b, 23b

Getty Images: 10, 11, 14, 84, 94, 154, 173t, 176

Jason Millet: 182

Library of Congress: 189

Mary Evans: 119, 148, 192

Naval History and Heritage Command: 36

New York Public Library: 92l

Rex Features: 113

Shutterstock: 6, 8, 16, 26, 40, 45, 47, 48, 51, 52, 54, 55, 57, 58, 59, 60, 62, 64, 66, 67, 72, 74b, 75, 77, 79, 80, 82l, 93, 95r, 96, 98, 103, 109, 110, 112, 114, 116, 117, 121, 122, 123, 124, 129, 130, 131, 135, 140, 142, 145, 146, 149, 153, 157, 158, 160, 161, 163, 165t, 166, 170, 173b, 174, 178 (x2), 183b, 193, 196, 197, 201, 202, 203, 204 (x2)

Shutterstock Editorial: 76

Wikimedia Commons: 18, 20 (x2), 22t, 25, 34, 35b, 38, 43, 44, 46, 49 (x3), 50, 61, 63, 65, 68, 74t, 78, 86, 87, 88, 89, 91, 92r, 95l, 99, 101, 104, 106, 107, 108, 118, 120, 125, 126, 127, 132, 136, 137, 139, 141, 155, 156, 162, 165b, 169, 177, 181, 183t, 184, 186, 187, 188, 191, 194, 198, 199